BEYOND BRICK AND MORTAR

Unveiling the Soul of India's Street Food

Foodity (P) Limited

CONTENTS

Section 1
IMPACT ON LOCAL ECONOMIES

In the bustling shade of civic life, where the thoroughfares are alive with the meter of steps and the symphony of honking cornucopias, there exists a culinary macrocosm that transcends borders and binds communities. Street food, with its attractive aromas and tasteful creations, is not just a shamefaced pleasure; it's an artistic show, a hoot of tastes that shifts and shimmers from one megacity to another. It's a narrative spun with vestments of diversity, affordability, and the sheer art of coming together at the collaborative table.

According to a report by FAO (Food and Agriculture Association) (2017), "there are around 2.5 million people who tend to eat road food daily. That's to say, the number of consumers of 'road food' is adding day by day. Also, Indian food is one of the most popular foods worldwide. They've a veritably different range of savors. They've quite a large range of spices admixed with food, giving a unique taste to every food item. There is large quantum of road food particulars in India that you can try, similar as paratha's, gol gappas, tandoori funk, kahthi rolls, bheil puri, aloo tikki, pakoras, samosas, kebabs, etc. They keep a long-lasting succulent flavor on the taste kids."

Embarking on a global trip through the alleys and avenues, we discover that each megacity boasts its own road food identity. From the racy appeal of Bangkok's Pad Thai to the savory aroma of Mumbai's Vada Pav, every road corner tells a story through its unique culinary innovations. Street food is not just food; it's a reflection of a megacity's soul, a living testament to the flavors that define its artistic twinkle. One of the charmsthat make road food a thick part of civic life is its availability.

In a world where dining out can be a luxury, road food emerges as the champion of the fund-friendly feast. Whether you are a pupil on a budget or a seasoned professional seeking a quick bite, the egalitarian nature of road food democratizes culinary gests, making gastronomic delights accessible to all. Beyond the flavors that dance on our taste kids, road food serves as a catalyst for a unique form of social commerce.

Picture this a bustling road corner, ambrosial with the aroma of grilling skewers and sweet spices. Then, people from all walks of life meet, each with a participated purpose – to savor the tasteful immolations of road merchandisers. Nestled in the complicate lanes of Chandni Chowk, where history whispers through ancient walls and the chaos of commerce mingles with the scent of spices, stands a culinary icon- Khan's Kebab Corner.

With its roots forcefully bedded in the fabled thoroughfares of Delhi, this fabulous road food joint has not just survived the test of time but has surfaced as a lamp, drawing patrons from far and wide to savor the flavors that have come an integral part of the megacity's gastronomic heritage. The story begins decades ago when a culinary visionary, Grandmaster Khan, set up a modest cube in the heart of Chandni Chowk. Armed with a treasure trove of family fashions and an unyielding commitment to perfection, he embarked on a charge to review kebabs. Each spice, strictly sourced, each condiment, a nearly guarded secret – Khan's Kebab Corner came the center of a gastronomic revolution in the bustling heart of Delhi.

What makes Khan's Kebab Corner an enduring gem in the culinary crown of Chandni Chowk? It is not just the excellence of the kebabs but the unchanging substance of the flavors. The fashions, passed down through generations, remain untouched by the winds of change. The Seekh Kebabs still bear the hand mix of spices, the Chicken Tikkas embody the perfect balance of tenderheartedness and housekeeper, and the iconic Roomali Rotis are as thin and scrumptious as ever. The patrons of Khan's Kebab Corner are not just guests; they're pilgrims on a gastronomic trip. Families return time after time, grandparents introduce their grandchildren to the magic of the kebabs, and musketeers gather to relive the recollections forged in the ambrosial alleyways of Chandni Chowk.

It's not just about the food; it's about the tradition, the history, and the participated joy of savoring flavors that defy the beach of time. The act of planning and meeting over road food is not just a matter of convenience; it's a festivity of participated moments. Families, musketeers, and indeed nonnatives find themselves drawn to the informal charm of road-side beaneries. In this casual setting, exchanges flow freely, walls break down, and the shade of society is woven tighter.

Street food, with its humble origins, becomes the great equalizer, bridging gaps and forging connections that extend beyond culinary boundaries. As we cut the globe through the lens of road food, we discover not just the different flavors that metropolises offer but the vestments that bind communities together. Street food is further than a gustatory experience; it's an artistic miracle that celebrates diversity, affordability, and the simple joy of participating a mess. In the midst of sizzling grills and sweet spices, we find a world where palates and people unite, transubstantiating each road corner into a collaborative dining table and every bite into a participated memory.

Join Aayat, a spirited food discoverer, as she unravels the vibrant shade of India's road food, where each state boasts its own unique flavor symphony. From the savory thoroughfares of Mumbai to the robust aromas of Delhi's heartiest' Chole Bhature,' Aayat's culinary trip becomes a thrilling lift through the distinctive tastes that define each region. In Mumbai, she finds comfort in the iconic' Vada Pav' and succumbs to the pungent appeal of' Pav Bhaji,' while Delhi introduces her to the art of heartening road feasts with its notorious' Parathas.' A sweet caper through Kolkata reveals the tasteful secrets of' Rosogolla' and the infectious charm of' Kathi Rolls.' Aayat also navigates south to Chennai, where' Idli- Sambar' and' Masala Dosa' reign supreme, and to Goa's littoral delights featuring' Prawn Balchão' and' Fish Curry Rice.' In each state, road food becomes not just a culinary experience but an artistic adventure, weaving together flavors that leave an unforgettable mark on both taste kids and hearts. As she aptly puts it," India's road food is a festivity of diversity, a gastronomic trip that brings people together through the magic of flavors. It's not just about what you eat; it's about the stories told with each bite, a succulent reflection of our rich culinary heritage."

Dive into this scrumptious passage with Aayat, where every road bite is a passport to a new state and a new adventure in taste.

In the lively thoroughfares of India, where the symphony of sizzling kissers orchestrates a succulent preamble, the impact of road food on original husbandry unfolds as a scrumptious narrative. Then, road food merchandisers aren't just culinary crafters; they're profitable maestros, shaping communities and weaving affordability into every tasteful morsel.

Micro-Entrepreneurs and Affordable Feasts:

Take a perambulation through the vibrant lanes of Chandni Chowk, and you will encounter original merchandisers who have perfected the art of delivering not just taste but affordability. According to a recent study by the National Street Food Association, these micro-entrepreneurs contribute significantly to the original frugality, creating a robust informal sector. Picture this a cheerful seller adroitly casting' Pani Puri,' offering five pungent explosions in crisp puris for a bare 20 rupees. This is not just road food; it's an profitable ballet where merchandisers come micro-entrepreneurs, making succulent mouthfuls accessible to all. The affordability quotient is not just a pricing strategy; it's a commitment to icing that the savory delights of Indian road food are within reach of everyone, anyhow of their profitable status.

Supply Chain Dynamics and Pocket- Friendly

Pleasures Drone into the bustling thoroughfares of Mumbai, where the' Vada Pav' merchandisers do not just serve a snack; they produce a fund-friendly revolution. These original icons not only give a scrumptious respite but also contribute to a dynamic force chain cotillion. According to a report by the Ministry of Agriculture, the harmonious sourcing of fresh vegetables, sweet spices, and ethereal pav chuck by these merchandisers stimulates the original frugality, creating a multiplier effect. The profitable ripple effect is not just theoretical; it's palpable in the pockets of the merchandisers, the original growers, and, most importantly, the eager guests enjoying a budget-friendly feast.

Social Tapestry and Affordable Indulgences

Beyond the economics, road food merchandisers paint a pictorial social shade by offering affordable indulgences. In the bustling requests of Ahmedabad, a' Pani Puri' seller becomes the neighborhood's culinary minstrel, offering five rounds of scrumptious explosions for a fund-friendly sum. A recent check conducted by the Civic Sociology Department at a leading university highlights how these collaborative tables, set amidst the ambrosial chaos, are where people from different walks of life unite over affordable delights. Then, profitable deals come moments of participated joy, and affordability transforms into a currency that binds communities together.

A Symphony of Affordability and Flavor

Consider the 'Chole Bhature' merchandisers in Delhi, where a storming plate of this North Indian delicacy is not just a culinary treat but an affordable luxury. For as little as 50 rupees, locals and callers likewise can delight the mouthwatering combination of ethereal bhature and racy chickpeas, creating not just a mess but a collaborative experience. In the southern lanes of Bangalore, the' Masala Dosa' merchandisers bring affordability to the breakfast table. A crisp, golden dosa filled with sweet potato masala, served with coconut chutney and pungent sambar, is a gastronomic delight available for a humble 30 rupees. The seller not only fills tummies but also adds a gusto of profitable vitality to the neighborhood. And as the sun sets in the littoral megacity of Kolkata, the aroma of' Kathi Rolls' airs through the air. Priced at a provident 60 rupees, these rolled delights filled with succulent flesh or paneer, come not just a road food item but a testament to the affordability bedded in the artistic fabric of the megacity.

So, the coming time you find yourself enchanted by the aroma of Indian road food, flash back that you are not just indulging in a culinary adventure; you are partaking in an profitable ballet where affordability and flavor harmonize. From the budget- friendly' Pav Bhaji' booths to the humble 'Vada Pav' merchandisers, and from the racy 'Chole Bhature' in Delhi to the crisp' Masala Dosa' in Bangalore, road food in India is not simply about taste; it's a festivity of availability. It's a memorial that profitable impact can be as savory as the mouthfuls offered at 5 kissers for 20 rupees or a plate of 'Kathi Rolls' for 60 rupees – a succulent testament to the fact that, in the world of Indian road food, affordability isn't just a pricing strategy; it's the twinkle of the community, making the succulent shade of flavors accessible to one and all.

associated with preparing and selling the food is crucial. Subtracting these costs from the total revenue provides the gross profit, which can then be used to estimate annual earnings.

Record-Keeping and Expense Tracking: Street vendors need to keep track of their expenses, including permits, licences, equipment, and any other operational costs. Subtracting these costs from the revenue can provide a more accurate net profit estimate.

Observation and Experience: Experienced street food vendors often develop an intuition for estimating revenue based on years of observation and experience. They may factor in changes in customer behaviour, market trends, and other external factors.

Peer Comparison: Vendors may compare their performance with that of peers in similar locations or with similar offerings. This can provide insights into the competitive landscape and help in setting realistic revenue expectations.

It's important to note that these methods are often used in combination, and the accuracy of the estimate depends on the vendor's diligence in tracking sales and expenses.

Additionally, external factors such as changes in regulations, economic conditions, and local events can also impact revenue. Now let's have a look at some of the people who are a part of the street food industry.

Meet Santosh, a dedicated individual from Uttar Pradesh who has been running a mobile stall named 'Kanpur ke Chote Samose' for the past eight years, delighting customers with his mini samosas. What makes Santosh truly remarkable is his unwavering commitment to his daughters' education. Unlike some business owners who meticulously estimate their revenue, Santosh has a unique approach. He doesn't crunch numbers or keep tabs on earnings. Instead, every rupee earned from his stall is channelled directly into supporting his family. His bank account may not boast substantial figures, but that doesn't deter him. Whatever he earns is promptly invested back into the stall, ensuring a steady flow of crispy delights for his customers.

And what about his income? Well, it's the simple joy of knowing that whatever remains after covering expenses is a testament to his hard work and dedication. Santosh's commitment goes beyond financial gains; it's about investing in a brighter future. So, the next time you savour one of Santosh's mini samosas, remember that you're not just enjoying a tasty treat—you're part of a heartwarming journey supporting family aspirations. Cheers to Santosh, his delicious samosas, and the smiles he brings to the taste buds! You can find his stall near Sehgal Pastry Shop, Lajpat Rai Chowk, Block E, Krishna Nagar, Delhi.

Now, let's meet Gagandeep, the heart and soul behind "Momos Point - Famous Maggi Vala" in Krishna Nagar, Delhi. For a whopping 15 years, Gagandeep has been dishing out the most delightful momos and mouthwatering maggi from his lively stall. Gagandeep's business approach is fairly simple. He is not one to get bogged down by spreadsheets or comparisons, just the joy of serving up delicious eats. His revenue estimates are more like a casual nod to the deliciousness he puts out into the world, rather than a meticulous number-crunching affair. And when it comes to banking, Gagandeep's trusty bank account is there for the everyday stuff, handling the regular payments from his satisfied customers. It's a no-fuss, customer-focused approach that keeps things rolling smoothly.

So, the next time you find yourself at "Momos Point - Famous Maggi Vala", know that you're stepping into a slice of Delhi's culinary legacy, sprinkled with the simplicity and warmth that Gagandeep brings to every plate. Here's to 15 years of momo magic and maggi bliss!

1.2 What percentage of your income is reinvested in the local community (e.g., sourcing ingredients locally, hiring local staff)?

Street food vendors across India don't just serve up delectable dishes; they are often deeply woven into the fabric of their local communities. A notable aspect of their operations is the concerted effort many make to source their ingredients locally, creating a symbiotic relationship between their businesses and the community.

Consider the journey of a typical street food vendor who begins their day by strolling through nearby markets. Here, they carefully select fresh produce from local farmers, not only ensuring the quality and freshness of their ingredients but also actively contributing to the livelihoods of those within their community. Spices, an essential component of many street food recipes, often find their way into vendors' kitchens from local spice merchants and specialty stores. This not only adds an authentic touch to their offerings but also sustains the vibrant spice businesses within the vicinity. Some vendors go beyond routine market visits, establishing enduring relationships with local suppliers. This collaborative approach not only guarantees a consistent supply chain but also strengthens the local economic ecosystem. A significant aspect of this practice is the homage paid to cultural and culinary heritage. Street food vendors frequently draw inspiration from regional traditions, using locally sourced ingredients to create dishes that reflect the diversity of India's culinary tapestry.

The support doesn't stop at ingredients; street food vendors actively engage with local businesses. They acquire bread from nearby bakeries and seek out specialty items from neighbourhood shops, contributing to the success of small enterprises and sustaining a vibrant local economy. Beyond economics, the impact extends to the environment. By sourcing locally, vendors inadvertently reduce their carbon footprint. The shorter transportation distances not only benefit the environment but also align with a broader commitment to sustainability. The relationship between street food vendors and their local communities goes beyond a transactional exchange. It's a nuanced interplay of community engagement and mutual support. As vendors tailor their offerings to suit local tastes, the food becomes a shared experience that binds the community together.

In essence, when you savour that flavorful street food, you're not just enjoying a culinary delight; you're partaking in a community-driven experience. It's a testament to the nterconnectedness of food, community, and the diverse tapestry of local businesses that make each neighborhood distinctive. Let's see how some of the street food vendors give back to their community–Santosh, 'Kanpur ke Chote Samose' stall from Uttar Pradesh, has a strategy that reflects both savvy business sense and a deep commitment to his community. Picture this: he dedicates one-third of his daily earnings to source his every day ingredients. As for ingredients, he not only taps into the local treasures of Uttar Pradesh but also frequents nearby stores. This not only ensures the fresh and fine ingredients but, as a bonus, helps him dodge hefty transportation costs.

The remaining two-thirds of his income is a blend of family care and a commitment to trust. He doesn't trust anyone with his delightful mini samosas. Instead, he's chosen to keep it close to home by hiring someone from his own city.

Similarly, Gagandeep, the owner of "Momos Point - Famous Maggi Vala" in Krishna Nagar, Delhi, where the aroma of momos and maggi has been enchanting taste buds for the past 15 years. When it comes to managing the funds from this culinary haven, Gagandeep follows a 40:60 or 60:40 ratio.In simpler terms, for every rupee earned, 40-60% mingles its way back into the stall, ensuring that the magic continues to unfold. It's a blend of business acumen and a passion for serving up the best to the loyal customers who make "Momos Point" a cherished spot in Krishna Nagar.

1.3 Have you noticed any changes in local economic activity (e.g., increased foot traffic, new businesses near your street food stall?) Please describe.

Navigating the bustling streets and sizzling griddles, street food vendors are like culinary wizards with a keen eye on the pulse of economic activity. Just when they whip up your favourite treats, they're also subtly attuned to the rhythms of the local economy. It's not only about serving up delicious bites but also about reading the treet-level economic vibes.

So, how do these street food maestros notice changes in the economic activities around them?

Navigating the bustling streets, street food vendors are like seasoned observers of the economic dance around them. Picture this: they effortlessly read the ebb and flow of foot traffic, sensing the hustle during payday weekends and the quietude on holidays. Without jotting down a single note, these patterns become their real-time economic scorecard.

Regular customers, those trusted souls, become conduits of local economic whispers. Conversations with vendors reveal insights into new job opportunities, shifts in spending habits, and the general buzz about town. Vendors attune their ears to these friendly exchanges, absorbing valuable information.

Masters of pricing intuition, street food vendors feel the economic breeze—whether customers are tightening their belts or embracing a willingness to splurge. Adjusting prices or offering specials becomes their way of harmonising with these economic nuances.

Fluctuations in ingredient costs act like signals in the culinary stock market. Street food vendors, sharp analysts in their own right, swiftly make adjustments to maintain the delicate balance, ensuring there's something to take away for both the customer and their pockets.

The weather isn't mere small talk for street food vendors; it's a key player in the economic dynamics of the day. Rain, shine, or the first breeze of autumn, changes in weather patterns influence customer turnout, impacting sales and offering a weatherman's forecast for the economic day.

In the digital dance, street food vendors are adept at noticing trends on social media platforms. They pick up on what's buzzing, what's not, and skillfully adjust their offerings accordingly. It's akin to having a finger on the pulse of the virtual economic landscape.

A unique challenge for street food vendors is the arrival of new competitors. The trumpet of a new business can either threaten their regular customer base or bring an opportunity for new food varieties. This keeps the vendors alert, prompting them to strategize on maintaining their standards in the face of fresh competition.

In the is a bustling market of live economic flow. It's a dance where vendors and customers share the stage, creating a dynamic that goes beyond the transactional. Let's find out how different street food merchants handle this level of economic activity around them.

Let's look at some of the street food vendors– Santosh, the owner of the Kanpur ke Chote Samose stall in Krishna Nagar, Delhi has a widespread fame drawing people not just from neighbouring towns like Haridwar, Ghaziabad, and Haryana but also people who host different social gatherings bring in bulk orders for him. Even those visiting Delhi for a brief stint make a point to indulge in his delectable samosas, including students about to embark on their overseas journeys who savour his treats for the last time before leaving. This way they keep experiencing a regular increase in the footfalls from the nearby places as well as from the faraway towns.

The same way, Gagandeep from the Momos Point-Famous Maggi Vala keep up with their regular and loyal consumers. They also entertain a huge number of people who come from the organic promotions through social media just to indulge in their delicacies. And, as per the stall owner, the number of people never decreases at their stall, it's always an onwards and upwards number.

Section 2

FOOD SAFETY PRACTICES IN STREET FOOD

In the chaotic thoroughfares of Delhi, where the hustle and bustle produce a symphony of civic life, there exists a culinary macrocosm that captures the substance of India's different flavours – road food. The tantalizing aroma of spices, the swish of grills, and the vibrant colors of road- side booths draw localsand callers into an alluring world of gastronomic delights. Fromthe ambrosial alleys of Chandni Chowk to the lively requests of Mumbai, Indian road food stands as a testament to the country's rich culinary heritage.

India, with its myriad societies, languages, and geographies, boasts a road food culture that glasses its diversity. In the narrow lanes of Kolkata, the sweet air of' Jhal Muri' being set –a creation of puffed rice, spices, and chutneys – resonateswith the artistic sprightliness of the megacity. In the southern state of Kerala, the aroma of 'Sulaimani Chai' airs through the air, accompanied by the sizzling sound of banana galettes, offering a unique mix of flavors that reflects the region's spice- laden history.

Move further north to Amritsar, and the iconic' Amritsari Kulcha' takes center stage. Stuffed with racy potato stuffing and cooked in tandoors, this Punjabi delicacy embodies the robust and hearty flavors of the region. Meanwhile, in the western state of Gujarat, the thoroughfares come alive with the swish of 'Dabeli' – a racy potato admixture-boxed in a soft pav, sprinkled with pomegranate seeds and sev, creating a pleasurable emulsion of textures.

As we carouse in the show of Indian road food, it's essential toadmit the enterprises that lurk beneath the face. The appeal of road- side delectables frequently prompts questions about the cleanliness of implements, the quality of constituents, and the general hygiene practices embraced by the culinary crafters orchestrating this symphony of flavors. In the heart of Old Delhi, where 'Chole Bhature' merchandisers battle for attention, the rapid-fire pace of food medication raises queries about the conscientiousness of hygiene in these bustling kitchens.

The iconic' Pav Bhaji' booths of Mumbai, though celebrated for their scrumptious immolations, also invite scrutiny regarding the source and running of constituents in open- air requests. The water used in the medication of' Pani Puri' – a popular road food enjoyed across the country – becomes a focal point of concern, egging a near examination of the safety of this ubiquitous road- side delight.

Meet Aisha, a spirited food sucker with a partiality for exploring the retired gems of Indian road food. For her, each road corner is a new chapter staying to unfold, filled with the tantalising aromas of spices and the pledge of culinary adventures. One scorching autumn in Jaipur, Aisha set up herself drawn to the lively chaos girding a' Pav Bhaji' cube, seduced by the pledge of a scrumptious escape from the mundane.

As she approached the bustling cube, the vibrant medley of colors and the symphony of sizzling bhaji kissers-heightened her expectation. A cheerful seller, slipping a vibrant apron, saluted her with a smile that spoke volumes about the passion bedded in his culinary craft. Intrigued but conservative, Aisha could not help but wonder about the hygiene norms of this roadside haven.

To her surprise, the seller's station was a well-orchestrated cotillion of cleanliness. His hands, sheathed in plastic gloves, moved with the perfection of a seasoned cook. The implements lustered under the sun, a testament to the seller's commitment to cleanliness in the heart of the bustling road. Aisha's original enterprises began to dissipated she observedthe scrupulous care with which the seller handled constituents, icing a flawless mix of flavors without compromising on hygiene.

Driven by curiosity, Aisha struck up a discussion with theseller, hoping to uncover the secrets behind his culinary success. The seller, whose name was Raj, participated perceptivity into the strict food safety practices he followed. Rajemphasized the significance of sourcing fresh yield daily, maintaining a strict routine of cleaning and disinfecting implements, and clinging to the hygiene norms set by the original health authorities.

As Aisha savored the first spoonful of the sweet' Pav Bhaji,' she realized that the flavors dancing on her palate weren't only a result of Raj's culinary prowess but also a reflection of his unvarying commitment to hygiene. The racy, pungent notes amalgamated-seamlessly, leaving her not just satisfied butalso comforted about the safety of her road- side indulgence.

Inspired by Raj's fidelity, Aisha continued her culinary capers across different metropolises, each road food hassle turning into a particular-disquisition of hygiene practices. Whether it was the' Chole Bhature' in Delhi or the 'Dhokla' in Ahmedabad, Aisha discovered a common thread – the obscure icons behind the road food booths who, like Raj, converted their roadside trials into lights of flavor and cleanliness.

Aisha's trip through the show of Indian road food not only heightened her appreciation for different flavors but also shattered preconceived sundries about the hygiene of road- side delectables. Each experience came particular evidence to the culinary crafters who, with their commitment to cleanliness, turned the chaotic thoroughfares into an immersive shade of safe and savory delights. And so, Aisha's culinary adventures continued, fueled by the consolation that the world of Indian road food wasn't just about taste; it was a festivity of flavor, culture, and unwavering hygiene norms.

2.1 How do street food vendors in different regions of India approach hygiene and food safety practices?

Street food vendors across different regions of India exhibit a diverse range of approaches to hygiene and food safety practices, influenced by local culinary traditions, cultural norms, and adherence to regulatory standards. Here's a nuanced look at how these vendors navigate the complex landscape of ensuring both flavor and safety:

Local traditions and Practices

In Delhi and Amritsar of North India, vendors crafting 'Pani Puri' and 'Chole Bhature' blend traditional practices with modern standards, emphasizing the use of fresh produce and meticulous cleanliness. Meanwhile, in the southern realms of Chennai and Hyderabad, the art of fermenting dosas and idlis is accompanied by a commitment to regular cleaning rituals. The bustling street food scene in Mumbai and Ahmedabad of West India mirrors a delicate balance between spice-laden flavors, like 'Vada Pav' and 'Pav Bhaji,' and stringent cleanliness. Over in East India, Kolkata's 'Kathi Rolls' and 'Puchka' vendors prioritize the use of clean water and sanitary storage.

Regulatory Compliance:

Licensing and Registration: Street food vendors are required to obtain licenses or register with local health authorities, following the guidelines set by the Food Safety and Standards Authority of India (FSSAI). This regulatory framework varies across states but generally involves inspections to ensure compliance with hygiene standards.

Training and Awareness: Many vendors undergo food safety training programs, educating them about the importance of hygiene practices. Certification in food safety is encouraged, and some regions may have local initiatives to raise awareness about safe food handling.

1.1 How do you estimate your annual revenue from street food vending business?

Estimating annual revenue for street food vendors in India can be a challenging task, as it often involves various factors and uncertainties. Here are some common methods that street food vendors may use to estimate their annual revenue:

Daily Sales Tracking: Street food vendors often keep a daily record of their sales. By tracking the number of items sold and their prices, they can calculate daily revenue. Over time, they can average these daily figures to estimate monthly and annual revenue.

Foot Traffic and Location Analysis: Vendors may consider the foot traffic in their location and the potential customer base. Busier areas with more people passing by are likely to generate higher sales. Vendors in prime locations may charge slightly higher prices.

Seasonal Variations: Street food sales can be influenced by seasons. Vendors may experience higher sales during festivals, holidays, or favourable weather conditions. Analysing seasonal variations helps in estimating annual revenue more accurately.

Customer Loyalty and Repeat Business: Street food vendors who have a loyal customer base may estimate revenue by factoring in the frequency of repeat business. They might consider regular customers and the likelihood of them returning for more purchases.

Cost of Goods Sold (COGS) Analysis: Understanding the cost of ingredients, packaging, and other expenses

Innovative Solutions:

Use of Technology: In certain urban areas, street food vendors leverage technology for online hygiene ratings and customer reviews. This transparency encourages vendors to maintain high standards to attract more patrons.

Innovative Equipment:

Vendors may invest in modern, easy-to-clean equipment, acknowledging the need for both efficiency and cleanliness in their operations.

Community Engagement:

Customer Trust: Maintaining customer trust is paramount for street food vendors. Regular patrons often develop a relationship with vendors, fostering an environment where hygiene practices become an integral part of the vendor's reputation.

Local Communities:

In close-knit communities, vendors may adhere to communal norms, ensuring that the preparation and serving of street food align with cultural expectations of cleanliness.

In essence, the approach to hygiene and food safety among street food vendors in India is multifaceted. It blends traditional practices, regulatory compliance, innovative solutions, and community engagement, creating a dynamic and evolving landscape where the pursuit of flavor harmonizes with the imperative of safety.

Meet Raj, a street food vendor in Jaipur. In the labyrinth of competing stalls, Raj's commitment to hygiene sets him apart. His innovative use of technology, like online hygiene ratings, reflects a modern approach. One day, a skeptical customer, Aisha, approached Raj's 'Pav Bhaji' stall. Intrigued by the spotless utensils and the transparency of Raj's ratings, Aisha took a bite. The explosion of flavors and Raj's dedication to cleanliness won Aisha over, showcasing how vendors like Raj blend tradition and innovation for an unforgettable street food experience.

In this diverse culinary landscape, regulatory compliance, innovative solutions, and community trust merge, creating an engaging narrative where the pursuit of flavor coexists with the imperative of safety.

Dive into the runners of time, where India's thoroughfares unfold a racy tale of road food elaboration – a story sprinkled with masala, artistic custodians, entrepreneurial tang, and a gusto of literal drama.

The Chaat Chronicles

Imagine the ancient stores of India, where the aroma of spices allured empty souls. These were the cradles of road food, where merchandisers in bustling requests cooked treats that would tantalize taste kids. Picture the lively thoroughfares of ancient Varanasi, where' Pani Puri' might have had its humble onsets, or the ambrosial bylanes of Old Delhi, where' Chole Bhature' fashions were rumored from one generation to the coming. Fast forward through time, and these thoroughfares witnessed the elaboration of road food from original delights to a global gastronomic miracle.

The Street Kitchens of Kolkata

In the heart of Kolkata, where the air is thick with the swish of road-side kissers, road merchandisers were not just culinary maestros; they were the artistic custodians, passing down fashions like treasured patrimonies. suppose of the iconic Kathi Rolls that began in the complicate thoroughfares of Kolkata, where merchandisers converted into entrepreneurs, balancing tradition with a sprinkle of invention. The formerly humble' Phuchka' wain evolved into a mobile kitchen, a oil for culinary trial that brought forth new flavors while keeping the substance of the thoroughfares alive.

The Mumbai Vada Pav Revolution

As the sun set over the Arabian Sea in Mumbai, a culinary revolution brewed on its thoroughfares. merchandisers went from tattling out' Pav Bhaji' under the megacity lights to transubstantiating into culinary entrepreneurs. The formerly simple' Vada Pav' wain came a mecca of creativity, serving up a mix of flavors that echoed the spirit of Mumbai – presto- paced, different, and unapologetically bold.

Spicy Challenges in the thoroughfares of Chandni Chowk

Yet, this masaledar trip isn't without its challenges. In the complicate thoroughfares of Chandni Chowk, where history meets flavor, safety enterprises have always been part of the narrative. From the Mughal period to the bustling present, the narrow lanes echoed with worries about cleanliness and the sourcing of constituents.

The road food merchandisers, amidst the chaos, continued to weave their magic, conforming to changing times and strict safety guidelines. As we tromp through this masala- laden tale of Indian road food, from the ancient stores to the bustling thoroughfares of moment, the narrative is a heady blend of tradition and invention, a festivity of original flavors and the entrepreneurial spirit that defines every road corner. So, let's savor the masaledar drama, delight the literal flavors, and celebrate the vibrant road food culture that has left an unforgettable mark on every gali and nukkad in India.

Picture the spice requests of Old Delhi, where merchandisers apply masalas like wizards casting spells. The medication of road food in India is an intricate cotillion of spices – a symphony where every component has its part. From the earthy cumin in' Aloo Tikki' to the fiery red of chili greasepaint in' Bhel Puri,' the thoroughfares are a palette of flavors. merchandisers, draped in the sprightliness of their masala- stained aprons, come maestros, balancing the precise mix of spices that define the soul of their culinary creations. It's a craft passed down through generations, a witchcraft that turns humble constituents into gastronomic treasures.

In the narrow lanes of Kolkata's road requests or the chaotic alleys of Mumbai's food havens, the sourcing of constituents is a saga in itself. Street food merchandisers in India are scrupulous about the newness and quality of their yield. The vegetable requests come their stalking grounds, where the merchandisers, armed with canny eye for perfection, choose the juiciest tomatoes for' Pav Bhaji' or the crispest coriander for garnishing' Chaat.' It's not just about buying constituents; it's a ritual, a connection with the source that elevates the road food experience to a culinary passage.

The road- side kitchens of India are a theater of fizzes, aromas, and culinary theatrics. Take the' Jalebi' seller in Varanasi, adroitly curling the batter into hot oil painting, creating golden gyrations of agreeableness. Or the' Kathi Roll' maker in Kolkata, adroitly flipping rolls on a hot griddle, investing the air with the scent of spices. The' Puchka' seller in Chandni Chowk becomes a juggler, filling crisp shells with a racy creation on demand. Each seller is a culinary artist, learning the nuances of their craft, from the nippy toss of a' Dosa' in Chennai to the metrical whack of a spatula on a hot tawa in Mumbai. cuisine styles aren't just about preparing food; they are a performance, a cotillion that captivates the senses. Beyond the swish of kissers and the sweet swirls of spices, the heart of India's road food culture lies in the intimate cotillion between merchandisers and guests.

It's a relationship woven with familiarity, badinage, and a participated love for flavors. Picture the' Chai Wala' in Jaipur, who knows each client's preferred mix of spices and agreeableness, or the' Pav Bhaji' seller in Mumbai who remembers every regular's choice of redundant adulation. It's not just a sale; it's a moment of connection. The road seller becomes a fibber, participating tales of their culinary heritage, the secret behind a hand dish, or the alleviation behind a new creation. The client, in turn, becomes part of the narrative, contributing to the ever- evolving story of India's road food.

Now, let's cut the different geographies of India, where each region boasts its own culinary shoptalk. In Delhi, the thoroughfares reverberate with the swish of' Kebabs' and the scent of' Chole Bhature,' while Kolkata's bylanes are a festival of' Kathi Rolls' and' Phuchkas.' Move south to Mumbai, and you are ate by the tempting aromas of' Vada Pav' and' Pav Bhaji.' The bustling requests of Chennai offer a symphony of spices in every' Dosa' and' Idli.' It's not just about the variety of dishes; it's about the unique flavors that synopsize the spirit of each region. In the alluring thoroughfares of India, road food is further than a craft; it's a festivity. It's the cotillion of spices, the symphony of fizzes, the badinage between merchandisers and patrons, and the emulsion of tradition with invention. It's a masaledar trip that captivates the taste kids and weaves a narrative of culinary art that's uniquely Indian. So, let's savor the flavors, delight the stories, and celebrate the rich culinary craft that makes India's road food a feast for the senses.

Now, let's cut the different geographies of India, where each region boasts its own culinary shoptalk. In Delhi, the thoroughfares reverberate with the swish of' Kebabs' and the scent of' Chole Bhature,' while Kolkata's bylanes are a festival of' Kathi Rolls' and' Phuchkas.' Move south to Mumbai, and you are ate by the tempting aromas of' Vada Pav' and' Pav Bhaji.' The bustling requests of Chennai offer a symphony of spices in every' Dosa' and' Idli.' It's not just about the variety of dishes; it's about the unique flavors that synopsize the spirit of each region. In the alluring thoroughfares of India, road food is further than a craft; it's a festivity. It's the cotillion of spices, the symphony of fizzes, the badinage between merchandisers and patrons, and the emulsion of tradition with invention. It's a masaledar trip that captivates the taste kids and weaves a narrative of culinary art that's uniquely Indian. So, let's savor the flavors, delight the stories, and celebrate the rich culinary craft that makes India's road food a feast for the senses.

FSSAI laid down hygiene and safety standards specifically tailored for street food vendors, acknowledging the unique challenges they face. The guidelines cover everything from the sourcing of ingredients to the storage, preparation, and serving of street food.

Picture the 'Puchka' vendor in Kolkata, where FSSAI mandates the use of clean water for the preparation of the tangy concoction that fills the crispy shells. In Mumbai, where 'Vada Pav' rules the streets, FSSAI guidelines ensure that vendors adhere to strict hygiene practices in the preparation of the potato filling and the chutneys. These standards become a culinary constitution, a set of rules that aim to preserve the rich tapestry of flavors while safeguarding the health of eager patrons.

As the regulatory drama unfolds, it begs the question – how effective are these regulations in ensuring the safety of India's street food? The answer is as masaledar as the street food itself. While FSSAI has made significant strides in creating awareness and establishing standards, the effectiveness of mplementation varies across regions. In the bustling markets of metropolitan cities, where the flow of tourists and locals converges, adherence to regulations is often more stringent. However, in smaller towns and crowded neighborhoods, the enforcement of guidelines encounters its share of challenges.

The real effectiveness lies not just in the regulations themselves but in the implementation and awareness among street food vendors. Initiatives like training programs, certification drives, and technological interventions, such as online hygiene ratings, contribute to creating a culture of compliance. The challenge lies in striking a delicate balance – ensuring safety without stifling the vibrant, spontaneous spirit of street food.

As we navigate the spice-laden streets of India, the regulatory frameworks become a backdrop to the culinary theatre. They are the silent guardians, ensuring that the 'Pav Bhaji' in Mumbai or the 'Chaat' in Delhi is not just a burst of flavors but a safe, memorable experience. The journey is ongoing, and as India's street food continues to evolve, so too will the regulations – a masaledar saga where flavor and safety dance in harmonious rhythm.

As the sun sets over the chaotic expressways of India, where the symphony of honking cornucopias and drooling crowds fills the air, road food merchandisers embark on a culinary adventure fraught with challenges. One of the foremost challenges is maintaining hygiene amidst the hustle and bustle. In the confined diggings of road- side kitchens, merchandisers grapple with limited space, water failure, and the absence of proper sanitation installations.

Picture the' Pav Bhaji' dealer in Mumbai, expertly stirring the racy creation on a small range, girdled by eager guests. The challenge also is not just the drug but ensuring that the tools, shells, and ingredients remain free from adulterants. also, in the bustling expressways of Old Delhi, where 'Chole Bhature' reigns supreme, merchandisers face the uphill task of managing the hygiene of their hands, tools, and the constant aqueduct of guests. Riding these challenges becomes indeed more critical during the rainstorm season, when the expressways transform into a watery maze. merchandisers battle not only the rudiments but also the trouble of waterborne adulterants affecting the safety of their offerings. Maintaining freshness amid the chaos is an art, and merchandisers are the obscure artists of this culinary ballet.

Yet, amid the challenges, street food vendors in India showcase a remarkable resilience and ingenuity. Let's unravel some case studies that exemplify the innovative solutions adopted by these culinary maestros.

In the Pink City, where the scorching sun often dictates the rhythm of life, a 'Chaat' vendor turned to innovation. By incorporating solar panels on his cart, he not only addressed the challenge of power supply for his equipment but also utilized the excess energy to run a water purification system. Clean water became the secret ingredient in his 'Pani Puri,' earning him a loyal customer base and setting an example for sustainable practices.

In the coastal city of Chennai, a 'Dosa' vendor took a bold step towards environmental sustainability. Frustrated by the environmental impact of disposable plates, he shifted to serving his delectable 'Masala Dosas' on banana leaves. This not only reduced the waste generated by his stall but also added a traditional touch to the dining experience. Customers embraced this eco-friendly approach, proving that innovation can be both practical and planet-friendly.

In the narrow bylanes of Kolkata, where 'Kathi Rolls' are an art form, a vendor faced the challenge of maintaining hand hygiene. He ingeniously crafted a mobile handwashing station, complete with soap and water, to ensure that both he and his customers could cleanse their hands before enjoying the flavorful rolls. This innovation not only elevated the hygiene standards but also became a unique selling point for his business.

One of the most fascinating aspects of India's street food culture is the delicate dance between creativity and safety requirements. Street food vendors are not just culinary artisans; they are also innovators, constantly pushing the boundaries of traditional flavors while ensuring the safety of their patrons.

Take the 'Bhel Puri' vendor in Mumbai's Juhu Beach, who introduces a new twist to the classic snack every season. From mango-infused 'Bhel' during the summer to a spicy 'Diwali Special' version, his creativity knows no bounds. Yet, he meticulously follows safety guidelines, ensuring that the freshness of ingredients and hygiene standards remain uncompromised.

Take the 'Bhel Puri' vendor in Mumbai's Juhu Beach, who introduces a new twist to the classic snack every season. From mango-infused 'Bhel' during the summer to a spicy 'Diwali Special' version, his creativity knows no bounds. Yet, he meticulously follows safety guidelines, ensuring that the freshness of ingredients and hygiene standards remain uncompromised.

Similarly, in the bylanes of Varanasi, where 'Jalebi' is an art, vendors experiment with shapes, sizes, and even flavors, introducing innovations like saffron-infused Jalebis.' The challenge lies in maintaining the traditional taste while embracing creative flair, striking a balance that captivates taste buds without compromising safety.

The 'Chole Bhature' vendors in Delhi's Chandni Chowk exemplify this delicate balance. While experimenting with innovative stuffing options for the Bhaturas, they remain vigilant about the cleanliness of their utensils and the quality of the cooking oil. The fusion of creativity and safety becomes a culinary philosophy, creating an ever-evolving menu that surprises and delights patrons.

As we savor the diverse flavors of India's street food, the challenges faced by vendors become part of the narrative. Their ability to innovate not only ensures the survival of their businesses but also enriches the culinary landscape. The sizzle of pans, the wafting aromas, and the inventive spirit of street food vendors create a tapestry where each bite is a testament to their resilience, ingenuity, and the masaledar magic that defines India's street food culture.

Meet Lakhan, a street food vendor in the bustling heart of Mumbai, where the chaotic streets become a stage for his culinary performance. Lakhan's 'Vada Pav' stall, tucked in a corner near a busy train station, is not just a culinary haven but a testament to his resilience and innovative spirit.

Lakhan, with a weathered apron and a twinkle in his eye, embarked on his street food journey a decade ago. Like any street vendor, he faced the daily challenges of maintaining hygiene amidst the ceaseless flow of customers. Mumbai's monsoon rains brought an added layer of complexity, turning the streets into rivers and the stalls into islands. Yet, he refused to let these challenges dampen his spirit.

His breakthrough came when he decided to embrace solar power for his humble stall. With a solar panel mounted on the roof of his cart, Lakhan not only solved the perpetual power supply issue for his equipment but also utilized the excess energy to power a small water purification system. Clean water became the cornerstone of his 'Pav Bhaji' and 'Vada Pav' preparation, transforming his street-side haven into a beacon of innovation.

Lakhan's solar-powered cart became a local sensation, attracting curious customers intrigued by the eco-friendly initiative. The aroma of his piping hot 'Vada Pav' wafted through the air, inviting patrons not just for a quick bite but for a glimpse into Lakhan's inventive world. The mobile handwashing station attached to his cart further underscored his commitment to hygiene, creating a sense of trust among his loyal clientele.

But Lakhan's innovations didn't stop there. In the spirit of Mumbai's dynamic culinary landscape, he introduced seasonal twists to his menu. From a 'Mango Madness Vada Pav' during the summer to a 'Diwali Delight Bhaji' in the festive season, Lakhan's creativity knew no bounds. Each innovation was a carefully crafted blend of tradition and modern flair, offering a unique experience for his patrons.

One day, Aisha, a tech-savvy customer, approached Lakhan's stall with her smartphone in hand. Intrigued by the online reviews praising Lakhan's cleanliness and innovative approach, she showed him a feature on a food rating app that allowed customers to scan a QR code for real-time hygiene ratings. Lakhan, ever the forward-thinker, readily embraced the idea. He displayed a QR code prominently on his cart, inviting customers to scan and witness the transparent hygiene standards he maintained.

Aisha, impressed by the fusion of tradition and technology, became a regular at Lakhan's stall. She not only savored the flavorful 'Vada Pav' but also became a loyal advocate for his business. Lakhan's journey, from a humble street food vendor facing challenges to an innovator embracing technology, reflects the essence of India's street food culture. It's a tale where each bite tells a story, and each customer becomes a part of the culinary narrative woven by the street-side artisans like Lakhan.

The first page of our culinary roadmap introduces a compilation of recommendations and best practices aimed at enhancing street food safety. It's a collaborative effort that draws from the collective wisdom of health authorities, vendors, and culinary enthusiasts.

1. **Hygiene Training Enterprise**

   Initiate comprehensive hygiene training programs for road food merchandisers. These programs, conducted in collaboration with health authorities and culinary experts, should cover

   stylish practices in food running, outfit sanitation, and particular hygiene. Practical, hands- on sessions can empower merchandisers with the knowledge and chops necessary to elevate safety norms.

2. **Accessible Sanitation Installations**

   Address the challenge of limited access to sanitation installations by uniting with original authorities to establish mobile or collaborative sanitation stations. icing that merchandisers have accessible access to clean water and sanitation installations is abecedarian to maintaining hygiene in road food medication.

3. **Technology-Driven Monitoring**

Grasp technology as a tool for real- time monitoring of road food safety. Introduce apps or platforms that allow guests to give feedback and rate merchandisers grounded on hygiene norms. similar technological interventions not only empower consumers but also produce a transparent system that encourages merchandisers to uphold safety practices.

Let's embark on a dialogue with the key stakeholders in India's street food narrative – the vendors, health authorities, and culinary experts.

In the vibrant markets of Delhi, we sit down with street food vendors to understand their challenges and aspirations. Raj, the solar-powered 'Vada Pav' vendor from Mumbai, shares his thoughts. "Hygiene is at the heart of what we do. We welcome training programs that equip us with the latest practices. Accessible sanitation facilities would be a game-changer for us. It's not just about serving delicious food; it's about ensuring our customers trust the safety of what we offer."

Dr. Gupta, a health official deeply involved in street food safety initiatives, emphasizes the need for collaborative efforts. "We're committed to ensuring the well-being of both vendors and customers. By working hand-in-hand with vendors, providing them with the tools and knowledge needed, we can create a safer street food ecosystem. Technological solutions for monitoring can offer a transparent, community-driven approach to ensuring compliance."

Chef Meera, renowned for her culinary expertise, believes in balancing tradition with innovation. "Street food is a cultural treasure, and safety measures should enhance, not stifle, its vibrant spirit. Integrating technology, like online hygiene ratings, can be a powerful motivator for vendors. But let's not forget the importance of community engagement – a collective commitment to fostering a safe and flavorsome street food experience."

The Role of Technology, Community Engagement, and Education:

1. **Technology as a Catalyst:**

    Imagine a Mumbai street buzzing with the latest tech innovations. Customers scan QR codes for real-time hygiene ratings, vendors receive alerts on their smartphones for upcoming training sessions, and health authorities monitor compliance through a centralized platform. Technology acts as a catalyst for transparency, accountability, and continuous improvement.

2. **Community Engagement:**

    Street food is not just about vendors and customers; it's a community celebration. Establishing local street food associations, where vendors collaborate with residents, health officials, and culinary experts, fosters a sense of community ownership. Regular meetings, events, and campaigns create a shared responsibility for maintaining hygiene standards.

3. **Education Initiatives:**

Education becomes the cornerstone of our strategy. Launch campaigns to educate both vendors and customers on the importance of hygiene. Interactive workshops, informative pamphlets, and community events ensure that everyone is on the same page. By empowering vendors with knowledge and instilling awareness in customers, we pave the way for a safer and more enjoyable street food experience.

As we envision the future prospects of street food safety in India, it's not just about regulations and guidelines; it's about fostering a culture where safety is ingrained in the vibrant tapestry of street food. Through collaboration, education, and technological advancements, we embark on a journey where each 'Pav Bhaji' and 'Pani Puri' is not just a delight for the taste buds but a testament to a community-driven commitment to safety and culinary excellence.

Section 3
CULTURAL SIGNIFICANCE OF STREET FOOD

Street food is such a vibrant part of culture, isn't it? It's like every bite tells a story of traditions, community gatherings, and the everyday life of a place. When you think about it, street food isn't just about the flavors, but also about preserving a slice of history and heritage. It's a way for people to maintain and share their culinary traditions from generation to generation. Additionally, it's a great window into the local lifestyle for travelers and food enthusiasts alike. The key takeaway is that street food is a living museum of cultural heritage, constantly evolving yet rooted in history. It's amazing how much you can learn about a culture just by exploring its street eats!

Indian street food is a vibrant symphony of flavors and textures, showcasing a wide array of mouthwatering delights enjoyed in public spaces. From the tantalizing 'Pani Puri' in Mumbai to the sizzling 'Chole Bhature' in Delhi, street food in India is an exquisite art form that reflects the country's diverse culture. It's not just about satisfying your taste buds; it's a sensory expedition that delves deep into the essence of Indian cuisine, where every dish narrates a tale of tradition, innovation, and togetherness.

In addition to its culinary marvels, Indian street food embodies the essence of 'chaat', spontaneous conversations and the vibrant ambiance of bustling marketplaces. It encapsulates the savory essence of history and heritage, offering a captivating journey into the intricate tapestry of Indian culinary diversity.

Street food, a ubiquitous and integral part of many cultures worldwide, has a rich and diverse history that dates back to ancient times. The concept of street food is not a novel one; it has been around since the advent of civilization when the first urban towns and cities began to form. Ancient markets, bustling with traders and vendors, were the precursors to the modern street food culture we know today. These markets were not just places for buying and selling goods, but they were also social hubs where people gathered, interacted, and, importantly, ate. The food sold in these markets was simple, affordable, and catered to the busy urban dwellers who needed quick and convenient meals.

As trade routes expanded and civilizations grew, the practice of selling food in public spaces evolved and diversified. The Silk Road, for instance, was not just a conduit for the exchange of goods, but also ideas, cultures, and cuisines. Traders and travelers along these routes brought with them their unique food practices and ingredients, influencing and shaping the local street food culture in the places they visited. This period marked a significant evolution in street food practices, with the introduction of new flavors, cooking techniques, and food items.

Prepare to embark on an awe-inspiring odyssey through the annals of time in India, where the mesmerizing tapestry of street food unfurls, mirroring the ever-evolving societal landscape. Immerse yourself in the ancient scriptures that whisper enchanting tales of 'Bhojanalayas,' the precursors to the bustling eateries of today, where people from all walks of life converged to partake in joyous communal feasts. As we fast forward, we find ourselves transported to the majestic Mughal era, where the streets pulsated with the tantalizing

sizzle of kebabs and the intoxicating aroma of biryanis, as the Mughal emperors lavished their culinary opulence upon the vibrant streets.

In India, the impact of cultural exchanges and migrations is etched into the very fabric of street food. The 'Samosa,' with its Central Asian origins, found a second home on Indian streets, while the 'Jalebi' and 'Gulab Jamun' trace their roots to Persian and Turkish influences. The centuries-old trade routes brought not only spices but also culinary techniques that continue to shape Indian street food today.

Cultural exchanges during the Delhi Sultanate and Mughal rule left an indelible mark on the culinary landscape. The introduction of kebabs, biryanis, and the iconic 'Kathi Roll' became emblematic of a gastronomic fusion that seamlessly blended Indian spices with Central Asian flavors. The streets of Lucknow, Delhi, and Hyderabad bore witness to the birth of these culinary marvels, becoming veritable museums of history and tradition.

In essence, Indian street food reflects the incredible diversity of the subcontinent, where every bite tells a story of conquests, migrations, and the amalgamation of culinary traditions. As you navigate the bustling markets and winding alleys of India, you're not just savoring food—you're experiencing the living history of a nation, where each street vendor becomes a custodian of centuries-old culinary legacies.

India, a land of diverse cultures, languages, and landscapes, boasts a rich tapestry of street food that varies dramatically from region to region. Each corner of this vast subcontinent contributes its unique flavors, ingredients, and culinary techniques to the vibrant mosaic of Indian street food.

Delhi, the pulsating heart of North India, is synonymous with a wide variety of chaats. From the tangy 'Pani Puri' to the spicy 'Aloo Tikki Chaat,' the streets of Old Delhi serve as a playground for chaat enthusiasts. The addition of hearty and flavorful 'Chole Bhature' vendors enhances the street food scene, creating a haven for those who crave the taste of North Indian gastronomy.

Step into the lively city of Chennai, where the bustling streets reverberate with the sizzling symphony of 'Dosa' being cooked on hot griddles. Indulge in the quintessential South Indian breakfast feast featuring soft and fluffy Idli, crunchy 'Vada', and the delectable combination of coconut chutney and tangy sambar. And to complete this culinary experience, relish a piping hot cup of South Indian filter coffee that will awaken your senses and set the perfect tone for the day ahead!

Dubbed as the 'City of Nizams,' Hyderabad beckons food enthusiasts with its majestic offering of the legendary 'Hyderabadi Biryani.' Within the lively markets, skilled street vendors skillfully prepare this aromatic rice dish, infusing it with a symphony of fragrant spices and succulent meat. The result is a culinary masterpiece that has become synonymous with the city, captivating the hearts and palates of all who indulge in its exquisite flavors.

Step into the lively streets of Ahmedabad and let your taste buds embark on a flavorful journey through Gujarat's culinary wonders. Treat yourself to the airy and spongy 'Khaman Dhokla,' a steamed cake crafted from fermented chickpea flour batter. Pair it with the irresistible crunch of 'Fafda,' a popular snack that perfectly complements the sweetness of 'Jalebi.' Whether it's a festive occasion or a regular day, this street food combination is sure to satisfy your cravings and leave you wanting more. Don't miss out on the chance to savor the authentic flavors of Ahmedabad!

In each region, Indian street food reflects not just culinary diversity but also the cultural, historical, and geographical nuances that define the subcontinent. The streets become the storytellers, sharing the tales of generations through the sizzling griddles, aromatic spices, and the joyous conversations that echo in every bite.

3.1 Let's have a look at what these places have unique to offer and how are they culturally significant

3.1.1 Kolkata is sometimes referred to as India's culinary capital and is the birthplace of the famous Kathi Rolls. Originally created as a convenient snack for Calcutta residents on the go, Kathi Rolls have come to represent the city's innovative food culture. Kathi

Rolls are prepared by cooking marinated chicken, mutton, or paneer kebabs on skewers, then wrapping them in a paratha and serving them with hot sauces and fresh onions. The end product is a portable pleasure that strikes the ideal balance between rich, buttery paratha, juicy meat, and smokey tastes. The combination of

Bengali and Mughlai cooking traditions is embodied in Kathi Rolls. They are more than just a street dish; they are a symbol of Kolkata's culinary scene's inventiveness and vibrancy. The busy streets with Kathi Roll vendors become a testament to the city's love for indulgent yet accessible gastronomy.

3.1.2   The unassuming but recognizable Vada Pav is the ideal street food companion for Mumbai, a city that is constantly on the go. The essence of Mumbai's fast-paced lifestyle is captured in this street food. Vada Pav is served with tamarind, mint, and garlic chutneys and a spicy mashed potato fritter between two pavs. Every bite of these delectable treats is a harmonious fusion of flavors and textures thanks to the expert assembly of the Vada Pav vendors. In addition to being delicious, Vada Pav is a cultural equalizer that is enjoyed by individuals from various backgrounds. The streets that are lined with Vada Pav stands turn become gathering places for Mumbaikars, who are all infatuated with this straightforward but filling street dish. It is more than just a snack; it is a phenomenon that reflects culture.

3.1.3   In addition to being the spiritual center of Sikhism, Amritsar is a gastronomic paradise known for its renowned Amritsari Kulcha. This city in North India is proud of its extensive culinary history. Amritsari Kulcha is a type of leavened bread that is filled with minced meat, paneer, or spicy potatoes. These Kulchas, when baked in tandoors, get a crispy outside and a soft inside. They are frequently served with a dab of butter and chole, or spiced chickpeas. Amritsari Kulcha is a cultural institution rather than just a meal. When the smell of freshly baked Kulchas fills the air, foodies from all over the world travel to Amritsar to experience the real Punjabi cuisine. Eating Kulchas together turns into a celebration of Amritsar's rich culinary heritage.

The streets of Kolkata, Mumbai, and Amritsar come alive in these case studies with the distinct tastes and cultural narratives that contribute to Indian street food's status as a dynamic and essential component of the nation's culinary identity.

The inclusiveness of street food is one of its most notable qualities. It establishes a fair playing field where individuals from different socioeconomic backgrounds come together. The streets provide a democratic environment where everyone can enjoy the culinary treats, regardless of whether they are curious tourists or locals. The varied people occupying the same space benefit from this inclusivity by feeling more connected to one another and sharing common experiences.

Street food dissolves barriers that frequently divide cultures, acting as a social equalizer. People from many walks of life stand shoulder to shoulder in these outdoor kitchens, bound by a shared love of delicious food. Even something as basic as waiting in line to enjoy a favorite street food can start spontaneous discussions and create bonds beyond social conventions.

Eating street food is more than just a means of survival; it's a ritual that's ingrained in local communities' daily lives. Street food becomes a cultural ritual—a shared activity that unites communities—whether it's the morning chai and samosa routine in India, the evening get-together at a taco stand in Mexico, or the late-night noodle slurping in Asian night markets. In local festivals and celebrations, street food assumes a central role, becoming an essential component of the ceremonial fabric. During festivals, food vendors filling the streets add to the joyous atmosphere in addition to providing a culinary extravaganza. Street food may be found everywhere from the colorful food stalls lining the streets of Rio de Janeiro during Carnival to the "Chandni Chowk Parathe Wali Gali" during Diwali in Delhi.

Lets meet Maya and know about her story. In the bustling city of Delhi, where the air is infused with the tantalizing aromas of spices, there lived a young woman named Maya. Maya, a curious soul with a passion for history, embarked on a journey to rediscover her cultural roots through the vibrant world of street food.

Maya's grandmother, a repository of culinary traditions, often regaled her with stories of the street food markets in Old Delhi—the narrow lanes adorned with colorful stalls, each narrating a tale of centuries-old recipes and culinary legacies. Intrigued by these tales, Maya set out on a quest to uncover the cultural significance embedded in the street food that had woven itself into the fabric of her family's history.

Her journey led her to the iconic Paranthe Wali Gali in Chandni Chowk, where generations of street food vendors had crafted delectable parathas for eager patrons. As she bit into a crisp, golden paratha filled with spicy potato filling, Maya felt a connection to the past—a taste that echoed the flavors her grandmother had described. The vendor, an elderly man with hands that danced over the griddle, shared stories of his ancestors who had perfected the art of paratha-making over decades.

Inspired by this encounter, Maya explored the bylanes of Chandni Chowk, each street offering a new chapter in the city's culinary history. At a chaat stall tucked away in a corner, she savored the burst of flavors from a plate of spicy and tangy aloo tikki chaat. The vendor, a jovial soul with a twinkle in his eye, explained how chaat had evolved from a royal Mughlai delicacy to a beloved street food cherished by locals and tourists alike.

Maya's culinary odyssey also took her to the vibrant Dilli Haat, where regional specialties from across India converged. Here, she sampled the succulent kebabs of Lucknow, the piquant pani puri from Mumbai, and the aromatic biryani from Hyderabad—all under the open sky, surrounded by the kaleidoscope of India's diverse culinary heritage.

As Maya immersed herself in these culinary experiences, she realized that street food was not just about flavors; it was a living testament to the cultural amalgamation that defined India. The street vendors, with their time-honored recipes and stories passed down through generations, became the custodians of cultural traditions.

Maya's journey was not just a gastronomic exploration; it was a discovery of her own identity. She found that the street food stalls were not merely places to satisfy hunger but thriving hubs where cultural practices, rituals, and stories converged. The shared tables became bridges connecting strangers, and the sizzling griddles carried the echoes of centuries-old culinary conversations.

With every samosa, dosa, and jalebi, Maya felt the pulse of her cultural heritage beating strongly. Street food, she realized, was not just sustenance; it was a living, breathing narrative of India's history, diversity, and resilience. And as Maya continued her journey through the labyrinth of Delhi's streets, she understood that the cultural significance of street food was not confined to the past—it was a vibrant celebration of heritage that continued to evolve, one delicious bite at a time.

The intersection of cultural preservation and safety in street food visioning demands a comprehensive and cooperative approach. A healthy street food ecosystem is built on recommendations that range from community engagement and education to technological integration and cooperative conversations. One can make sure that the colorful tapestry of street food not only survives but thrives, delighting future generations with its flavors, stories, and cultural diversity by establishing a symbiotic partnership between sellers, health authorities, culinary specialists, and the community.

Section 4

STREET FOOD AND TOURISM

The travel industry is changing rapidly, driven by an increasing number of adventurers who want more from their travels than merely sightseeing. They want a fully immersed experience that appeals to their senses and a connection to the local way of life. An unexpected hero, street food, is at the center of this dramatic change. Street food, which was once confined to the periphery of culinary discovery, has gained importance and is now a global magnet that attracts tourists from all over the world. This section delves into the development of street food, following its journey from modest origins to a worldwide phenomenon that influences the fundamental aspects of the travel experience.

With its roots in the heart of the community, street food has experienced a remarkable transformation. What was originally a straightforward way to survive in crowded marketplaces and tiny lanes has developed into a popular cuisine all across the world. Street food has become a cultural touchstone that invites travelers to immerse themselves in the colorful tapestry of a destination's culinary traditions as they look for more authentic experiences.

The rise in food tourism has brought street food to the forefront. Street cuisine is becoming an essential component that characterizes the core of a trip, rather than being restricted to the outside of travel itineraries. Today's tourists want to experience a destination's true flavor, aroma, and authenticity via all five senses, and street food offers the ideal opportunity to do just that.

Road food's appeal goes much beyond the act of eating; it develops into a symphony of tastes, scents, and cultural stories. Previously faceless individuals, street vendors now serve as the guardians of a place's gastronomic culture. For the discriminating tourist, street food creates a story that captivates the senses and leaves lasting memories, from the sizzle of a hot wok to the perfume of spices drifting through congested passageways.

Travelers are looking to street food markets and stalls as windows into a destination's spirit in their quest for authenticity. These food hotspots are more than just quick meal locations; they're flavor-filled living museums where every dish tells a tale of creativity, tradition, and the spirit of the community. The foundation for a thorough examination of how street food transforms and draws in contemporary tourists is laid out in this section.

Street food stands out as a worldwide magnet that links nations, overcomes borders, and turns routine travel into spectacular odysseys as the tourism industry shifts towards immersive and experience travel. This introduction lays the groundwork for a deeper exploration of the complex relationship between street food and tourism, enticing readers to go on a culinary adventure that explores travel beyond the surface and reveals the mysteries that lie within the enticing realm of street-side cuisine.

Street food is an unmatched means of experiencing a new culture when traveling, since experiences are the new currency. The sounds of skewers sizzling on an open grill, the aroma of spices wafting through busy markets, and the vivid colors of street-side stalls all entice visitors to engage in a more meaningful and genuine connection with a destination's soul, beyond the glossy brochures and well-traveled tourist paths.

With its diverse range of flavors and textures, street food goes beyond simple nourishment and takes on the role of a cultural ambassador, enticing visitors to partake in a culinary adventure deeply rooted in the customs and legacy of the area. Each dish has a backstory that goes much beyond the components that are placed on the plate. From the complex blend of spices in Indian chaat to the savory simplicity of Italian arancini, street food serves as a living testament to the rich tapestry of global gastronomy.

Travelers who explore neighborhood markets and street corners in search of these delectable treats discover that they are experiencing more than simply eating— they are also taking in the spirit of the destination. The street vendor takes on the role of a storyteller, imparting the background of each dish, the methods that have been handed down through the ages, and the significance of flavors that have endured. Travelers can taste the very essence of a destination through dining, which becomes a sensory experience that extends beyond sightseeing.

Street food is not just a great way to experience a new culture; it's also incredibly democratic, inclusive, and useful. Accessibility and affordability are two of its most alluring qualities, which make it a desirable choice for a wide range of tourists. Street food becomes the great equalizer in the complex dance of international tourism, where travel preferences and budgets differ greatly.

A thorough examination of numerous case studies and survey data reveals the critical roles that accessibility and affordability play in ensuring that street food is an inclusive dining experience. Vibrant kiosks along the sidewalks of major cities provide a common ground for travelers, be they luxury seekers with a flair for authenticity or backpackers on a tight budget. Street food's humble origins cut across socioeconomic barriers, guaranteeing that the joys of culinary exploration are not exclusive to a particular demographic.

Street food becomes a catalyst for removing boundaries, promoting diversity, and democratizing the culinary scene when viewed through the prism of affordability. It frees visitors from the confines of posh restaurants to interact with the local food culture. Street food's egalitarian vibe turns busy marketplaces into gathering places where people from all backgrounds come together to enjoy similar tastes and the excitement of trying new foods.

Moreover, street food accessibility encompasses not just financial factors but also cultural and physical accessibility. Street sellers are frequently found in the center of residential areas, far from popular tourist destinations. Because of its clever placement, tourists are encouraged to explore places they might not have otherwise considered visiting. As a result, visitors get a more genuine experience of a place's heartbeat, as locals and visitors come together to share a fondness for the delicious food served at street-side eateries.

In addition to its deliciousness, street food's appeal to tourists stems from its capacity to cross cultural barriers, give a true taste of the past, and offer a gastronomic experience that is affordable for everyone. It's a culinary equalizer that encourages visitors to actively participate in the dynamic global street food culture as well as to fully experience the authenticity of a destination.

Tourism centered around food is a prominent trend that has evolved in the ever-changing landscape of travel preferences, transforming the way tourists discover and interact with locations. The culinary experience is prioritized in this game- changing method of travel, and the magnetic appeal of Indian street cuisine lies at the center of this culinary journey. Indian street food takes you on a fascinating trip that goes beyond simple sustenance. It captivates the senses and turns a meal into an adventure.

Gastronomic tourism is not the same as the traditional idea of eating for survival. It represents the longing for a profound, immersing relationship with a place's culinary character, and Indian street cuisine is essential to satisfying this curiosity. Indian street cuisine sticks out as a beacon that draws visitors into the center of the local culture as they look to delve beyond the surface and connect with the true soul of a place.

This section explores the concept of Indian street food-driven gourmet tourism and how it can serve as a catalyst for an in- depth culinary journey. No longer satisfied with passive dining experiences, travelers actively seek out street food markets and vendors as hubs of exploration, turning a meal into a memorable journey that resonates long after the journey concludes.

With the global culinary renaissance taking place, certain Indian cities are positioning themselves as culinary tourist destinations by capitalizing on the allure of their street food scenes. This division looks at particular Indian cities that have not only embraced their street food culture but also developed it to the point where it is now a top draw for travelers from all around the world.

4.1 Culinary Tourism Hubs:

MUMBAI

Mumbai is an example of how street food can completely change a city and turn it into a destination for gastronomic travel. The vivid and disorderly street markets, like the well- known Khau Gallis, provide a sensory overload of tastes, smells, and cultural encounters. Travelers swarm to these busy streets for an intensive culinary trip through the heart of Indian cuisine, not simply for a quick snack. Mumbai's street cuisine, which includes the fiery Vada Pav and the delicious Pani Puri, not only enhances but also defines the vacation experience.

DELHI

Street food is more than simply a culinary experience in Delhi's huge metropolis; it's a cultural phenomenon. The city's street vendors create a tapestry of flavors that captures the depths of Indian cuisine, from the spicy Kebabs to the savory Chaat. Travelers looking for a true experience of Indian traditions are drawn to Delhi by its thriving street food scene, which is known for its kaleidoscope of colors and alluring aromas.

KOLKATA

Kolkata has cleverly positioned its street cuisine as an essential component of its appeal, given its historical charm and ethnic diversity. The lively marketplaces and well-known street food destinations, such as College Street and Park Street, are transformed into culinary extravaganzas with Bengali specialties like Jhalmuri, Puchka, and Kathi Rolls. Travelers are captivated by Kolkata's street food, which offers a sensory feast, in addition to its historical wonders.

These case studies highlight how Indian street cuisine has the power to elevate cities into international hotspots for culinary tourism. In certain places, Indian street food becomes more than just a side dish—it becomes a distinctive feature, a cultural icon that draws visitors from all over the world.

Essentially, Indian street food's appeal as a tourist draw comes from its capacity to go beyond the typical, providing a taste experience that extends beyond the plate.

It is an invitation to experience more than simply flavors; to become part of a trip that becomes ingrained in the destination's culture and makes a lasting impression on the taste buds of the traveler. With its alluring allure, Indian street cuisine elevates the dining experience to a profound exploration, delving deeper into a city's heart, its culture, and its culinary heritage with each bite.

When travelers navigate the energetic streets of their destinations, it's not just the historical sights or landmarks that provide an unforgettable impression—street food allows for gastronomic exploration and adventure that elevates the travel experience as a whole. A basic lunch can become a life- changing culinary adventure when you use street food as a portal to a world of sensations. This section shows how street food may transform travel experiences by revealing the rich tapestry of tales from tourists who have gone on culinary excursions.

Travelers discover the skill of street vendors creating the ideal Vada Pav—a spicy potato fry wrapped in a soft bun—in Mumbai's crowded markets. A symphony of aromas that transcends the palette is ignited by the first mouthful, leading to a cultural immersion and a connection with the beating heart of the city. We investigate these instances of gastronomic discovery—where street food transcends its practical use and becomes a symbol of the spirit of the place—through anecdotes and testimonies.

Another traveler, strolling through the colorful alleys of Delhi, gives in to the temptation of the fragrant Kebabs frying on open grills. Each taste of a culinary marvel becomes a chapter in their journey memoir, along with the fragrant spices and intermingling scents that bring people together. These first- hand accounts highlight the transformative potential of street food, transforming regular travelers into gastronomic explorers in search of more than simply nourishment but a sensory experience that embodies the spirit of their chosen location.

In addition to serving meals, street food vendors serve as cultural ambassadors, encouraging sincere conversations and community involvement. A Puchka vendor in Kolkata's winding lanes takes on the role of a storyteller, imparting the history and legacy that are contained in every bite. Insights into how these encounters go beyond transactional transactions and foster genuine moments of connection that enhance the travel experience can be gained through interviews with both tourists and sellers.

In the busy streets of Jaipur, an unusual form of interaction takes place when a group of tourists gather around a lassi vendor, fascinated by the traditional method of making this refreshing drink. The vendor tells tales of centuries spent perfecting the blend, serving as both a purveyor of drinks and a guardian of culinary customs. These interactions with street food sellers develop into cultural discussions that bridge linguistic and cultural divides, going beyond simple business dealings.

This section emphasizes the mutually beneficial relationship that exists between street food sellers and the tourists they serve, as seen through the prisms of local relationships and community engagement. It's more than just purchasing a snack here; it's about engaging in a communal activity where the vendor turns into a tour guide, sharing not just culinary knowledge but also a window into the life and spirit of the neighborhood. These opportunities for interaction help to weave a common story that strengthens the bonds between visitors and residents.

To put it simply, street food improves the visitor experience in ways other than just the culinary. It's about the stories that are weaved into every meal, the journeys that are taken on with every mouthful, and the sincere relationships that are formed between food vendors and tourists. Street cuisine turns eating into a social festival that enhances travel as a whole and serves as a channel for cross-cultural engagement.

While the allure of street food is undeniable, it comes with inherent challenges, particularly in the realms of hygiene and safety. This section confronts the potential pitfalls that may arise when street food and tourism intersect, shedding light on how destinations and vendors navigate these concerns to strike a delicate balance between the irresistible charm of street food and the well-being of tourists.

In the labyrinthine lanes of Varanasi, a city known for its spiritual vibrancy and street food delights, the challenge of maintaining impeccable hygiene becomes apparent. Interviews with local health authorities and vendors reveal the intricate dance between preserving culinary traditions and adhering to stringent safety standards. From the careful sourcing of ingredients to the implementation of modern food safety practices, this subsection unravels the complexities faced by destinations aiming to preserve the authenticity of street food while safeguarding the health of those who indulge in it.

Furthermore, the narrative expands to global contexts, addressing instances where hygiene and safety concerns have been successfully mitigated. Case studies showcase destinations that have implemented innovative solutions, suchas food safety certifications for vendors and the establishment of designated street food zones with enhanced sanitation measures. By dissecting both challenges and triumphs, this section provides a nuanced understanding of how destinations can navigate the intricate terrain of street food and tourism without compromising on safety.

Technology integration offers interesting prospects as India's street food culture continues to enthrall residents and visitors alike. Imagine using a smartphone app to lead you through the busy lanes of Delhi's Chandni Chowk while learning the backstories of each street food vendor. The software would guide you through the maze-like pathways. The main recommendations are on creating user-friendly apps that are customized for Indian cities, including local languages and offering functionalities like virtual gastronomic experiences, historical insights, and real-time vendor reviews.

In the bustling markets of Mumbai's Khau Gallis, augmented reality takes on a new dimension. Wearing AR glasses, visitors may experience an interactive journey through India's culinary heritage as the history of classic dishes comes to life. In order to maintain the authenticity of street food experiences while improving the overall exploration for tech-savvy tourists, collaborations between tech developers, local governments, and street food vendors in India can guarantee the seamless incorporation of technology.

Sustainable methods are crucial in India, where street food is not simply a dish but also a cultural identity. In order to preserve culinary legacy and promote responsible tourism, it is imperative that Indian local governments, tourism boards, and street food vendors collaborate. Imagine a scene where a cooperative effort guarantees trash reduction, environmentally friendly packaging, and community-based projects that support the city's sustainability goals on Jaipur's busy streets.

Guidelines and certifications for Indian street food vendors should be established in order to support sustainable practices and guarantee the survival of both the cities and their culinary heritage. Educational initiatives take on a shared duty when visitors actively engage in and support sustainable practices. This cooperative strategy, which has its roots in the cultural ethos of India, not only supports environmental objectives but also improves the whole street food experience for both residents and tourists.

In a nutshell a harmonic fusion of sustainability and technology is envisioned for the future of street food tourism in India. While collaborative activities ensure that he economic benefits of street food tourism coincide with India's commitment to cultural and environmental preservation, technological advancements specifically designed for the Indian setting can offer a richer exploration of culinary traditions. These suggestions act as a road map for an exciting, sustainable, and culturally enlightening trip through the mosaic of Indian street food, as the cuisine continues to make its way into the story of international travel.

In the intricate dance of street food and tourism, what emerges is a narrative that transcends the mere act of eating—it's a cultural journey, an odyssey that extends far beyond the boundaries of sustenance. Street food has metamorphosed into a potent cultural catalyst, shaping the very essence of the tourist experience. From the bustling markets of Southeast Asia to the vibrant food carts of Latin America, the allure of street food invites travelers to savor not just flavors but narratives, creating indelible memories that linger long after the journey concludes.

As we reflect on the labyrinthine streets of Delhi's Chandni Chowk or the lively night markets of Bangkok, it becomes clear that street food is not merely about consumption; it's an invitation to immerse oneself in the soul of a destination. The symphony of aromas, the kaleidoscope of colors, and the communal spirit of street food markets forge connections that go beyond cultural boundaries. Each bite becomes a passport to a different world, a sensory journey that encapsulates the essence of a place.

Our exploration has unraveled the multifaceted layers of street food, from its historical evolution to its role as a magnet for tourists worldwide. It has illuminated the challenges faced by vendors and destinations alike, from hygiene concerns to the delicate balance of tradition and technology. However, amidst these complexities, street food emerges as a unifying force—a universal language that speaks to the heart of every traveler.

Street food is not confined by borders; it's a global phenomenon that invites individuals to partake in a shared experience. The narrative of a street food vendor in Marrakech echoes the aspirations of a vendor in Mumbai, and the communal joy of sharing a meal transcends language barriers. In this conclusion, we celebrate the transformative power of street food—an art that goes beyond the confines of geographical boundaries and cultural nuances.

As we close this gastronomic journey, it's clear that street food is more than a culinary indulgence; it's a cultural tapestry, a universal invitation to explore the world—one bite at a time. It beckons travelers to embrace the unfamiliar, to relish the narratives woven into each dish, and to discover the profound connections that arise when sharing a meal with strangers. Street food, with its timeless allure, remains a testament to the fact that the most profound cultural exchanges often occur not in grand palaces or famous landmarks but in the humble yet vibrant corners of the world where flavors, stories, and people intersect.

Section 5
NUTRITIONAL VALUE OF STREET FOOD

The pull of street food is undeniable; there's nothing quite like it—the perfect balance of flavors, the sizzle of grills, and the fragrant dance of spices that tempts onlookers. Street food is a monument to the global appreciation of taste, as evidenced by the fiery chaats of Mumbai and the flavorful kebabs of Istanbul. It's an open invitation to discover a world of gastronomic possibilities where each seller curates a distinct flavor profile to entice taste buds and guarantee a delicious adventure.

In this section, we take in the complex tapestry of flavors and scents that characterize street cuisine in many Indian cultures. We delve into the complex and regionally distinctive flavors and aromas that add to the sensory experience of Indian street cuisine, from the spicy Kathi Rolls of Kolkata to the fragrant Pav Bhaji of Mumbai. We want to convey the spirit of each meal through detailed descriptions, showing how the fragrant symphony differs from the streets of Delhi to the coastal aromas of Goa.

Expanding upon regional quirks, we demonstrate how Indian street cuisine serves as a microcosm of the world's gastronomic variety. The combination of flavors in a Mumbai Vada Pav or the unique combination of spices in a South Indian dosa symbolizes the blending of several cultures. We look at how Indian street food vendors keep the authenticity of local food while deftly incorporating influences from around the world. We highlight the diverse range of cuisines found in India by citing instances such as the Indo-Chinese fusion found in Tangra, Kolkata, or the widespread appeal of Indian street foods.

Turning our attention to the taste artisans, we present Indian street food vendors as the guardians of distinctive flavor profiles. We explore the artistry involved in creating tastes that appeal to Indian palates, from the chaat vendors of Jaipur to the masala chai wallahs of Varanasi. We highlight how these suppliers integrate a feeling of cultural identity into their offerings through interviews and personal experiences. Indian street cuisine is a sensory experience because of the unique flavors that are preserved and presented by the vendor, who transforms from a food purveyor into a storyteller.

In the vibrant tapestry of global cuisine, street food stands out not only for its tantalizing flavors but also for its unique ability to break down socioeconomic barriers. This exploration delves into the multifaceted role of affordability in street food, unraveling its capacity to serve as a culinary equalizer. From the bustling streets of Delhi to the night markets of Mexico City, street food becomes a symbol f inclusivity, democratizing culinary exploration and showcasing the entrepreneurial artistry of street food vendors.

In the vibrant tapestry of global cuisine, street food stands out not only for its tantalizing flavors but also for its unique ability to break down socioeconomic barriers. This exploration delves into the multifaceted role of affordability in street food, unraveling its capacity to serve as a culinary equalizer. From the bustling streets of Delhi to the night markets of Mexico City, street food becomes a symbol of inclusivity, democratizing culinary exploration and showcasing the entrepreneurial artistry of street food vendors.

In many civilizations, there is a gastronomic split between socioeconomic levels because access to fine dining experiences is frequently expensive. Street food breaks down these barriers by offering delicious yet reasonably priced options, making it a transformational force. This section explores how street food can become a leveler by providing a wide variety of cuisines that appeal to individuals of different socioeconomic backgrounds. We investigate how street food accessibility promotes a sense of community and belonging as people from diverse economic backgrounds share the same culinary places through case studies and real-world examples.

Case Study: The Chaat Stalls of Mumbai

Mumbai's bustling streets are adorned with chaat stalls that attract everyone from office executives to college students. The affordability of a plate of Pani Puri or Bhel Puri makes these street-side delicacies a unifying force. Interviews with vendors and patrons provide insights into how these stalls become social equalizers, where people from diverse economic backgrounds converge to savor the same flavorful bites.

For those who may not have the resources to enjoy good dining, street food provides as an affordable entry point into the realm of gastronomic exploration. This section explores how street food stands can serve as a gateway to a world of flavors through the democratization of taste. Street food allows people explore new flavors without breaking the bank, from the wide variety of kebabs in Istanbul to the noodle stalls in Bangkok. We demonstrate how street food democratizes not just taste but also cultural experiences through trip accounts and interviews.

Street food vendors are not merely purveyors of affordable meals; they are culinary entrepreneurs who masterfully blend tradition with innovation. This section explores the entrepreneurial spirit that propels street food vendors to create unique, affordable offerings. From reinventing classic recipes to introducing innovative twists, street food vendors showcase a form of culinary artistry that adapts to evolving tastes while maintaining a focus on affordability. Through interviews with vendors and a deep dive into their creative processes, we uncover the stories behind iconic street food dishes that have become cultural staples.

Case Study: The Kati Roll Carts of Kolkata

Kolkata's streets are dotted with Kati Roll vendors who have transformed a traditional street food item into a global sensation. By blending regional flavors with a portable format, these vendors exemplify entrepreneurial artistry. Through interviews with Kati Roll vendors and customers, we explore how these street food entrepreneurs not only cater to diverse palates but also contribute to the economic vibrancy of the city.

n the tapestry of street food, affordability emerges as a golden thread that weaves together communities, transcending socioeconomic divisions. Street food vendors, with their entrepreneurial spirit, become architects of a culinary egalitarianism that invites everyone to the communal feast.

From breaking barriers to democratizing exploration, street food's affordability not only satisfies taste buds but also nourishes a sense of unity that transcends economic differences. This exploration showcases how street food is more than a gastronomic delight; it is a powerful force for inclusivity, bringing people together through the universal language of flavors.

Indian street food, a treasure trove of flavors, showcases a diverse array of nutritional profiles rooted in the country's rich culinary heritage. This subsection explores the nutrient-packed delights found in iconic Indian street food, from the protein-rich kebabs of Lucknow to the vitamin-laden Poha of Maharashtra. Through a cultural lens, we unveil the nutritional benefits ingrained in the ingredients, illustrating how Indian street food embodies a harmonious blend of taste and health. Insights from nutritionists and interviews with street food vendors provide a holistic understanding of the nutritional richness inherent in these culinary creations.

Case Study: The Nutrient-Dense Chaat of Varanasi

Embarking on the streets of Varanasi, we explore the nutritional density of the city's renowned chaat offerings. Interviews with vendors and nutrition experts shed light on how traditional Indian ingredients like chickpeas, yogurt, and spices contribute to the healthful aspects of street food, dispelling misconceptions and celebrating the nutrient diversity of Indian street fare.

Although many like the flavors of Indian street cuisine, health issues are a common topic of discussion. This section of the investigation explores popular complaints, covering topics like oil content, cleanliness, and possible health hazards related to consuming Indian street cuisine. We seek to present a balanced viewpoint that recognizes issues and emphasizes the beneficial nutritional features of various Indian street food options through a thorough analysis.

We look more closely at the thriving street food sector in Mumbai and the hygienic measures taken by vendors. Health inspectors, vendors, and customers were interviewed to provide insight into the measures implemented to guarantee food safety. Our goal in addressing and recognizing sanitary issues is to provide a thorough picture of the health situation regarding Indian street cuisine.

Empowering consumers to make informed choices, this section emphasizes the importance of mindful selections when indulging in Indian street food. Through practical tips and expert advice, we guide readers on how to navigate the Indian street food landscape with an awareness of nutritional considerations. From choosing tandoor-cooked options to incorporating regional diversity for a balanced meal, this subsection encourages a holistic approach to enjoying Indian street food without compromising on health.

Drawing on nutritional expertise specific to Indian cuisine, we provide readers with practical tips for making mindful choices while exploring street food markets. These tips encompass strategies for incorporating spices for health benefits, balancing various regional cuisines, and exploring vegetarian and vegan options, ensuring that the Indian street food experience is both delicious and health-conscious.

In the nutritional adventure of street food Indian cuisine, variety becomes essential to a well-rounded and gratifying meal. Through careful consideration of the subtleties, responsiveness to issues, and encouragement of deliberate choices, Indian street food becomes not only a sensory extravaganza but also a gastronomic journey that honors taste and health in a balanced partnership within the country's rich cultural fabric.

In the vibrant tapestry of Indian street food markets, a universal truth emerges – the joy of shared experience. This subsection unravels the communal nature of Indian street food, where strangers become companions over a shared meal. From the crowded lanes of Chandni Chowk in Delhi to the bustling markets of Kolkata, communal dining fosters a sense of camaraderie. Through interviews with patrons and vendors, we capture the magic of shared tables, where conversations flow freely, and barriers dissolve amidst the pleasure of savoring delectable Indian street food offerings.

Case Study: The Chaotic Unity of Mumbai's Vada Pav Stalls

Exploring the chaotic unity of Mumbai's Vada Pav stalls, we delve into how communal dining transcends language and social barriers. Interviews with locals and tourists reveal how the shared experience of standing by a street-side stall, indulging in the iconic Vada Pav, and exchanging smiles creates an atmosphere of togetherness, exemplifying the intrinsic community spirit of Indian street food.

Indian street food markets serve as cultural crossroads, where diverse backgrounds converge over shared meals, breaking cultural and social divides. This part of the exploration investigates how Indian street food becomes a catalyst for cultural exchange, where individuals from different walks of life embrace the opportunity to taste, learn, and appreciate each other's culinary traditions. Through anecdotes and real-life stories, we showcase instances where the act of sharing a meal becomes a powerful tool for fostering understanding and unity.

Cultural Exchange in Jaipur's Street Food

Havens In the vibrant streets of Jaipur, we witness how street food vendors and visitors engage in a cultural exchange. Through interviews with vendors, tourists, and locals, we unravel how the act of sharing a table and savoring diverse dishes becomes a bridge that transcends cultural differences, fostering a shared appreciation for the richness of India's culinary heritage.

Markets Beyond the confines of cultural and social labels, Indian street food markets stand as arenas for the celebration of shared humanity. This subsection explores how the act of coming together over Indian street food transforms strangers into a community. From the lively markets of Varanasi to the festive stalls of Jaipur, we capture moments where the celebration of shared humanity becomes palpable. Interviews with vendors and patrons showcase how, amidst the chaos and flavors, a profound sense of connection emerges, celebrating the shared experience of being human.

The Vibrancy of Kolkata's Puchka

Stalls In the lively Puchka stalls of Kolkata, we explore how shared humanity takes center stage. Conversations with vendors and customers reveal how the communal spirit thrives in the midst of the lively bustle, creating an environment where people from various backgrounds unite in celebration, embracing the shared joys of life and food.

Within the bustling lanes of India's vibrant street food markets, this section unveils captivating case studies that illuminate the nutritional stories crafted by Indian street food vendors. These are tales of innovation, health-conscious choices, and regional influences that define the nutritional landscape of Indian street food.

a. **Championing Nutrition in Mumbai's Dabeli Stalls**

In the iconic street corners of Mumbai, Dabeli vendors have rewritten the narrative of this beloved snack. Traditionally a carb-heavy indulgence, these vendors have embraced a health-conscious approach by incorporating a medley of nutrient-rich vegetables. Spinach, carrots, and beetroot have become the stars of the show, replacing the conventional potato filling. Interviews with innovative vendors reveal the meticulous process behind this transformation, aiming to strike a balance between the signature Dabeli taste and a healthier nutritional profile. This case study sheds light on how these vendors have become trailblazers, showcasing that street food classics can evolve to cater to modern nutritional preferences.

b. **Delhi's Tandoori Charisma: Grilled Goodness on the Streets**

Delhi's street food scene is synonymous with Tandoori delights, and this case study delves into the nutritional innovations by Tandoori vendors. Traditionally known for its smoky flavors and succulent meats, Tandoori cuisine has undergone a subtle yet significant transformation. Interviews with vendors showcase a shift towards leaner meats and the use of yogurt-based marinades, reducing fat content without compromising on taste. This nutritional reimagining not only aligns with contemporary health-conscious preferences but also underscores the adaptability of traditional street food to evolving dietary expectations. Delhi's Tandoori vendors exemplify how, through thoughtful adjustments, street food can remain true to its roots while embracing a more health-conscious approach.

c. **The Green Revolution in Jaipur's Street Snacks**

In the colorful streets of Jaipur, a group of street food vendors has embraced what can be called the "Green Revolution." These vendors have creatively infused regional herbs and greens into their snacks, elevating the nutritional profile of traditional favorites. Fenugreek, spinach, and other locally sourced greens have become integral components, adding not just vibrant hues but also nutritional benefits. Interviews with these vendors showcase the conscious decision to introduce these ingredients, not only for their taste-enhancing properties but also for their health benefits. This case study explores how Jaipur's street food vendors have turned traditional snacks into nutritious delights, contributing to a more wholesome and diverse street food landscape.

As we explore the nutritional narratives of Indian street food, understanding consumer perspectives becomes paramount. Consumer attitudes towards nutritional considerations in Indian street food are evolving, reflecting a growing awareness of health-conscious choices. Interviews with patrons reveal a nuanced approach, where taste remains paramount, but there's a noticeable shift towards seeking healthier options. The perception of street food as solely indulgent is giving way to a more balanced perspective, with consumers expressing an interest in vendors who prioritize nutritional value. This shift is not a rejection of the rich flavors synonymous with Indian street food but rather a desire for a harmonious blend of taste and nutrition.

In the bustling streets of Bangalore, vendors offering nutrient- enriched chaats have garnered attention. By incorporating superfoods like kale, quinoa, and flaxseed into traditional chaat recipes, these vendors appeal to a demographic seeking both the familiar taste of street food and the added nutritional benefits. Consumer interviews highlight the positive reception of such initiatives, showcasing an evolving mindset where nutritional considerations play a role in shaping street food preferences.

Various factors influence dietary choices in Indian street food markets, creating a mosaic of preferences. Interviews and surveys indicate that the diversity of street food offerings caters to different dietary needs. While some consumers prioritize vegetarian options, others seek protein-rich dishes or gluten-free alternatives. The influence of cultural and regional dietary norms is evident, with consumers making choices aligned with their culinary heritage. Additionally, accessibility and convenience play a crucial role, with consumers often opting for street food that aligns with their dietary preferences while being readily available.

Kolkata's street food scene, known for its diversity, exemplifies how factors like cultural preferences and dietary needs shape choices. From the iconic Kathi Rolls to Puchka stalls offering both spicy and sweet variants, consumers in Kolkata navigate a rich tapestry of options that align with their dietary preferences, reflecting the dynamic interplay between tradition and personal choice.

The relationship between taste, affordability, and healthiness forms the crux of consumer decision-making in Indian street food markets. Interviews highlight that taste remains the primary driver, with consumers seeking the explosion of flavors synonymous with Indian street cuisine. However, there's a discernible demand for affordability, especially among the youth and students. The intersection of affordability and healthiness is evident in the popularity of vendors offering nutrient-dense options at pocket-friendly prices, catering to a demographic that values both health and budget considerations.

Delhi's bustling street food corners showcase the delicate balance between taste, affordability, and healthiness. Vendors offering health-conscious twists to traditional favorites, such as grilled kebabs or fruit chaats with minimal sugar, exemplify how the fusion of these elements appeals to a broad consumer base. Interviews reveal that consumers appreciate vendors who prioritize health without compromising the affordability and taste that define the essence of Indian street food.

Consumer perspectives on nutritional considerations in Indian street food underscore a nuanced landscape where taste, affordability, and healthiness intertwine. The evolving mindset reflects a conscious effort to strike a balance, seeking vendors who align with nutritional preferences without sacrificing the vibrant flavors that make Indian street food a culinary adventure. As consumers navigate the diverse offerings, their choices become a testament to the intricate dance between tradition and contemporary dietary consciousness in the realm of Indian street food.

The journey through the nutritional narratives of Indian street food has unraveled a series of key findings that weave a comprehensive story. From Mumbai's Dabeli vendors championing nutrient-rich vegetables to Delhi's Tandoori maestros embracing leaner meats, and Jaipur's street snacks undergoing a green revolution – each case study highlights the dynamic interplay between tradition and nutritional innovation. Consumer perspectives, too, reflect a nuanced shift, with taste remaining paramount but an increasing awareness of health- conscious choices reshaping preferences. These findings showcase the adaptability and resilience of Indian street food, ensuring it remains not only a custodian of taste but also a reflection of contemporary dietary consciousness.

Indian street cuisine is a cultural phenomenon that captures the essence of a multicultural country rather than just being a culinary delight. Apart from its tastes, textures, and scents, street food has a multifaceted significance that encompasses social interactions, cross-cultural interactions, and financial gains. Strangers make friends over shared meals in this celebration of our common humanity. This holistic value is further enhanced by the sellers' innovative nutritional approaches, which guarantee that street food serves as a source of both enjoyment and nourishment. Street food is a lively contributor to India's social fabric and a custodian of culture, and its comprehensive value is highlighted by this.

Section 6

SUSTAINABILITY IN STREET FOOD

The street food sector contributes significantly to urban food culture by offering a wide range of customers quick and varied gastronomic experiences. But worries about how street food businesses affect the environment have made sustainable methods necessary. The present study investigates the sustainability strategies implemented by street food sellers, with a particular emphasis on waste management, local ingredient procurement, and mitigating environmental effect. This research attempts to provide light on the existing status of sustainability within the street food industry and offer suggestions for future development through a thorough review of case studies and empirical research.

A thriving and essential part of metropolitan culinary landscapes, the street food sector has developed over time to become a ubiquitous source of accessible and varied culinary experiences. Street food vendors, who hailed from busy marketplaces and corner stores, have evolved into gastronomic entrepreneurs, providing a wide range of mouthwatering selections to suit a wide range of preferences. This industry makes a substantial contribution to the global food economy in addition to enhancing the cultural fabric of cities.

The popularity of street food can be ascribed to its capacity to offer quick, easy, and tasty meals that frequently pay homage to regional cuisine and culture. Street food has come to be associated with an exciting and immersive culinary experience, whether it's because of the scorching street-side grills, the inviting displays of diverse tastes, or the fragrant spices drifting through the air.

Street food vendors, who are frequently sole proprietorships or small companies, are essential to satisfying the needs of the growing urban population. Their menu features everything from regional specialties to fusions with international influences, fostering a welcoming and varied culinary scene. Additionally, street food frequently serves as a link between neighborhoods, encouraging social contacts and adding to the diverse fabric of urban life.

Even while the street food business is still booming, the larger food services industry's growing worries about environmental sustainability also affect it. A growing body of research has examined how food-related activities affect the environment as urbanization quickens and consumer consciousness rises. Particularly, street food vendors have come under fire for their roles in the production of waste, use of electricity, and overall environmental impact.

The increasing use of single-use plastics, throwaway packaging, and ineffective waste management techniques linked to street food businesses have alarmed environmentalists and decision-makers. Concerns over resource depletion, carbon emissions, and deforestation related to ingredient sourcing have intensified the need for a sustainable transformation in the sector.

The conflict between street food's environmental effects and its widespread appeal has created a critical need for creative and sustainable solutions. Street food sellers, customers, and government agencies are among the many parties involved in the food supply chain that are realizing how important it is to embrace environmentally friendly practices in order to preserve the industry's future while reducing its negative effects on the environment.

Given these difficulties, the purpose of this research paper is to examine the sustainable methods used by street food vendors, with an emphasis on waste control, obtaining locally produced food, and lessening environmental effect. This study aims to provide important insights for the future of street food and to add to the continuing conversation on sustainable urban food systems by examining present behaviors and assessing their effects.

Foodies around the world have been enthralled with street food as they search for culinary treats on busy city streets. But beneath the bright hues and mouthwatering scents, there's a rising worry about this beloved culinary tradition's environmental impact. In order to bridge the gap between taste and sustainability, this study aims to identify the sustainable practices that street food vendors are currently implementing. It also sets out to evaluate these practices' effects on waste reduction, local sourcing, and environmental sustainability in general.

6.1 Exploring the Gastronomic Green Spectrum: Objective 1: Investigate the Current Sustainable Practices

Picture the dynamic street food vendor, skillfully crafting delicacies amidst a symphony of sizzling pans and aromatic spices. In the heart of urban hubs, these culinary artisans navigate challenges and opportunities to align their practices with sustainability. This objective aims to unravel the kaleidoscope of initiatives undertaken by street food vendors – from innovative packaging solutions to eco-conscious ingredient choices. Through interviews, surveys, and on-the- ground observations, we seek to paint a vivid portrait of the sustainable landscape within the bustling world of street food.

Objective 2: Evaluate the Effects on Local Sourcing, Waste Management, and Environmental Sustainability in General

We explore the effects of these sustainable projects in addition to their mouthwatering flavors and eye-catching appearances. Does a cleaner urban environment result from less packaging waste? Does the move to local sourcing promote biodiversity and community resilience? This goal examines the concrete implications of sustainable practices on local ingredient procurement, waste management, and environmental sustainability as a whole. Our goal is to quantify the environmental impact of these initiatives by using both quantitative analysis and real-world case studies.

As we go out on this investigation, picture the shift: street sellers turning into sustainability stewards who use their culinary delights to tell a story of change. This study invites readers to relish the tales of street food vendors at the vanguard of the culinary green revolution, surpassing the traditional confines of academics. Come along on our journey towards a future where street food is more resilient, tasty, and sustainable.

Sustainability in the food industry encompasses a multifaceted approach aimed at mitigating environmental impact, promoting ethical sourcing, and ensuring social responsibility. From farm to table, stakeholders are reevaluating and restructuring their practices to create a more sustainable and resilient food system.

Sustainable Agriculture:

Practices such as organic farming, agroecology, and precision agriculture are gaining prominence. These methods prioritize soil health, minimize the use of synthetic inputs, and foster biodiversity, aiming to create a regenerative relationship between agriculture and the environment.

Supply Chain Transparency and Responsible Sourcing:

Companies are increasingly recognizing the importance of transparent supply chains. Ethical sourcing of raw materials, fair labor practices, and reducing the environmental footprint of transportation are integral components of sustainable supply chain management.

Waste Reduction and Circular Economy:

he food industry is addressing the challenge of waste generation through strategies such as reducing food waste, recycling, and adopting circular economy principles. From manufacturing to retail, efforts are being made to minimize the environmental impact associated with packaging and disposal.

Energy Efficiency and Green Technologies:

Energy-intensive food processing and manufacturing are transitioning towards renewable energy sources. Adoption of green technologies, such as energy-efficient appliances and sustainable packaging, is becoming a key focus for businesses aiming to reduce their carbon footprint.

Relevance of Sustainability in Street Food Operations:

While the broader food industry grapples with sustainability challenges, the unique characteristics of street food operations introduce a set of considerations that demand tailored solutions.

Waste Management Challenges in Street Food:

Street food, often characterized by its convenience and portability, has been associated with increased single-use packaging waste. Sustainable waste management practices in street food operations involve the use of biodegradable materials, recycling initiatives, and educating consumers about responsible disposal.

Local Sourcing and Community Engagement:

Sourcing ingredients locally not only reduces the environmental impact associated with transportation but also fosters community engagement. Street food vendors collaborating with local farmers contribute to the vitality of regional food systems, support local economies, and offer consumers a connection to the origins of their food.

Reducing Environmental Impact in Street Food:

The dynamic nature of street food operations presents opportunities for reducing environmental impact. Energy-efficient cooking methods, such as solar-powered carts, and the use of eco-friendly packaging showcase innovative approaches to make street food more sustainable.

A thorough study strategy is used to combine the breadth of empirical data gathering techniques with the depth of case studies in order to fully understand the difficulties of sustainability in street food.

To reflect a range of geographic locations, cultural contexts, and operational scales within the street food sector, a selection of diverse case studies will be selected. This guarantees a sophisticated comprehension of the sustainable methods that street food vendors employ. Prominent instances could comprise suppliers employing inventive approaches to waste handling, advocates of regional procurement, and trailblazers in mitigating ecological footprint.

A combination of surveys, in-person observations, and interviews will be used to collect empirical data. In order to obtain a comprehensive understanding of sustainable practices, vendors, customers, and pertinent stakeholders will be included. Street food vendors will be the subject of structured interviews that will explore their goals, obstacles they have encountered, and the results of their projects. Customers will be given surveys to complete in order to determine their awareness of and preferences for sustainable street food options. Real-time insights on customer interactions and operational procedures will be obtained through on-site observations.

Participants' privacy and confidentiality will be rigorously protected. Informed consent will be obtained from all interviewees and survey participants, outlining the purpose of the study, the voluntary nature of their involvement, and how their data will be used.

Recognizing the diverse cultural contexts of street food, cultural sensitivity will be prioritized throughout the research process. Respectful engagement with vendors and participants will ensure that their perspectives are accurately represented.

Measures will be taken to minimize any potential harm arising from the research. This includes refraining from asking intrusive questions and ensuring that participants do not feel pressured to disclose sensitive information.

Data Analysis: Savoring the Juicy Insights

Qualitative and Quantitative Analysis of Collected Data:

Qualitative Analysis:

hematic analysis will be employed to identify recurring patterns, themes, and insights within the qualitative data. Open coding will be used to categorize responses and narratives, allowing for the emergence of in-depth understanding.

Quantitative Analysis:

Survey data will undergo statistical analysis using software like SPSS or R. Descriptive statistics will illuminate trends in consumer preferences and awareness levels regarding sustainable street food practices. Inferential statistics, such as correlation analysis, will explore relationships between variables.

Statistical Methods Employed:

Correlation Analysis:

Investigating potential relationships between variables, such as the correlation between consumer awareness and preferences for sustainable street food options.

Comparative Analysis:

Comparing the effectiveness of different sustainable practices across case studies, considering factors like waste reduction, local sourcing impact, and overall environmental footprint.

Regression Analysis:

Exploring the predictive power of certain variables on the success of sustainable initiatives among street food vendors.

This research methodology promises a rich and nuanced exploration of sustainability in street food, ensuring that both qualitative narratives and quantitative trends are captured and analyzed. The combination of case studies and empirical data collection methods promises to yield juicy, engaging insights into the multifaceted world of sustainable street food practices

In the quest for sustainability, the packaging of street food emerges as a critical focal point. Innovations in sustainable packaging materials are transforming the landscape, offering alternatives to traditional single-use plastics. From biodegradable materials derived from plant-based sources to compostable packaging made from agricultural waste, a myriad of options is reshaping how street food is presented and consumed. This section explores the exciting realm of eco-friendly packaging, showcasing materials that not only serve the purpose but also contribute to a greener future for street food.

However, the path to widespread adoption of eco-friendly packaging is not without challenges. Cost considerations, availability of materials, and resistance to change pose significant hurdles. Street food vendors, often operating on tight budgets, may find the initial investment in sustainable packaging a financial strain. Additionally, educating consumers about the benefits and proper disposal of these materials is crucial for successful implementation. Despite these challenges, the opportunities presented by eco-friendly packaging are immense. Enhanced brand image, compliance with changing regulations, and alignment with consumer preferences for sustainable practices all contribute to the allure of adopting eco-friendly packaging. This section delves into the dynamic landscape of challenges and opportunities, illustrating the potential for a shift towards more sustainable packaging practices in the street food industry.

Street food operations, often characterized by their mobile nature, face unique challenges in managing energy consumption. From food carts to portable kitchens, exploring energy-saving practices becomes imperative for reducing environmental impact. This section delves into the innovative approaches adopted by street food vendors to enhance energy efficiency. From the integration of solar-powered appliances to the optimization of cooking methods, the exploration of energy-saving practices showcases the potential for sustainable transformation within the dynamic world of street food.

Implementing energy-efficient practices in street food operations is not without its obstacles. Limited space, reliance on traditional cooking methods, and the need for cost-effective solutions present significant challenges. However, success stories abound, demonstrating that overcoming these challenges is indeed possible. This section highlights the implementation challenges faced by street food vendors and the strategies employed to achieve energy efficiency. By examining both the hurdles and triumphs, a comprehensive understanding of the feasibility and impact of energy-saving practices emerges.

The results paint a picture of the street food industry's sustainable practices. Key findings highlight the current level of sustainability in the sector, ranging from waste management measures to local ingredient procurement, packaging advancements, and energy efficiency. The key findings are briefly summarized in this part, which also presents a clear picture of the state of sustainability in street food.

The implementation of sustainable practices in street food businesses has far-reaching effects on the sector as a whole, going beyond environmental concerns. The possible effects of adopting sustainability on vendor profitability, customer perception, and the sector's overall resilience are examined in this section. The discourse encompasses economic, social, and environmental facets, providing a thorough examination of the revolutionary capacity of sustainable methodologies.

Section 7

SOCIAL AND COMMUNITY ASPECTS OF STREET FOOD

Street food, with its sizzling grills, aromatic spices, and vibrant displays, extends beyond being a mere culinary experience; it weaves a rich tapestry of communal and cultural connections. This introduction sets the stage for a flavorful exploration into the social dynamics embedded within the street food landscape, tracing its historical roots, and elucidating the research objectives aimed at unraveling the intricate threads that bind people, flavors, and communities.

Street food becomes a vibrant, social phenomena in the maze- like labyrinth of urban life, providing more than simply a fast bite. It turns city sidewalks into thriving culinary hotspots where various populations come together to share their distinct tastes and customs around the communal table. Street food is vividly portrayed as a shared cultural experience by the vibrant conversations, the tantalizing fragrances drifting through the air, and the rhythmic clang of cutlery. The street food scene, which spans culinary barriers to provide a place where varied groups meet, is embodied by anything from food carts and booths to pop-up markets.

India, a land of myriad cultures, languages, and flavors, boasts a street food landscape that is nothing short of a vibrant carnival of tastes and aromas. Beyond the bustling markets and chaotic streets, street food is deeply ingrained in the fabric of Indian communal life. It transcends regional differences, bringing people from diverse backgrounds together at the roadside stalls, creating a shared space where culinary diversity becomes a unifying force.

From the iconic chaat vendors of Delhi to the savory pav bhaji stalls of Mumbai's street corners, the Indian street food scene mirrors the social intricacies of the country. Each city, town, or village has its unique street food culture, reflecting the local tastes and traditions. Street food becomes a democratic culinary experience, accessible to people from all walks of life, creating a social equalizer where everyone, from the office- goer to the rickshaw puller, can savor the same flavors.

India's street food culture is a tapestry woven with threads of history, tradition, and community. Dating back to ancient times, the concept of street food finds mention in texts like the Arthashastra, where street vendors were an integral part of marketplaces. Over centuries, street food in India has evolved alongside the changing landscapes of empires, colonial rule, and post-independence urbanization.

Historically, street food vendors were the purveyors of local flavors, offering regional specialties that reflected the culinary diversity of India. The dabbawalas of Mumbai, with their lunchbox delivery system, epitomize the communal aspect of street food, connecting communities through the shared experience of home-cooked meals delivered to workplaces.

The scope includes comprehending how, in a global and varied society, street food serves as a catalyst for social cohesion and cultural interchange in addition to being a delectable gastronomic treat. Our goal is to explore the various ways that street food vendors foster social cohesion by establishing forums for conversation, engagement, and exchange of experiences.

Indian urban narratives revolve around street food, whether it is found in the bustling metropolises of Delhi, the bustling bazaars of Kolkata, or the vivacious streets of Chennai. In the Indian setting, where traditional social structures are being reshaped by urbanization, it is imperative to comprehend the social and communal components of street food. Street food bridges socioeconomic gaps and creates a sense of belonging in the sprawling urban areas of a nation where cities are melting pots of cultures and groups.

Anthropologists have attempted to unravel the cultural meaning of street food, lured in like taste buds to a bustling marketplace. The structuralist method of renowned anthropologist Claude Levi-Strauss sheds light on the Indian environment. In addition to providing nourishment, he viewed street food as a symbolic system—a culinary language that encapsulated the core values and beliefs of a society.

Street food is more than just a transaction when we examine these scholarly viewpoints; it's a cultural artifact that's a physical representation of the customs, rituals, and stories that unite communities. Eating street food becomes more than just a means of subsistence; it's a way for people to connect and share a common language, history, and sense of identity.

Think of the crowded streets of Old Delhi, where the noise of the sellers blends with the scent of spices. This is where an academic narrative comes to life: the story of how Indian street food culture is a living anthropological lesson rather than just a matter of taste. The chaat seller transforms into a storyteller in the tiny lanes, conjuring up tales with each dash of chutney and pinch of masala. The street food cart becomes a hub of culture, where the study of taste becomes a sensory exploration of a community's common past.

The transformative effect of street food in shaping and reinforcing communal identity is reflected in the literature surrounding culinary storytelling as a means of fostering community. When food vendors line the streets, these areas become gathering places for people from all walks of life to enjoy delicious meals together. Street cuisine in India has a special ability to bring people together across linguistic, cultural, and economic barriers since the country celebrates diversity. Research indicates that street food vendors frequently take on the role of community identity keepers.

When we delve into the literature, we discover a wealth of research that examines the cultural customs and practices that are interwoven with the eating of street food. The tea merchant, or chai wallah, has a key role in everyday rituals in the Indian culture. Drinking chai turns from a quick refreshment break into a social ritual that promotes interaction and creates a forum for discussion.

Imagine a bustling Mumbai street where the seller selling vada pav transforms into a community resilience storyteller. The vada pav endures despite changing cultural norms and economic problems. The literature reflects the feelings of people who congregate around the modest stand, appreciating it as a communal hub as well as a location for quick bites—a monument to the power of a community's culinary story.

The body of literature on the anthropology of street food and its function in fostering community gives a clear picture of the deep bonds that are created over shared meals. It demonstrates how street food is more than simply a business deal; it's also a forum for cultural exchange, an investigation into anthropology, and a gathering place where a variety of narratives are shared. The sections that follow this research will further explore and analyze these flavorful connections, uncovering the layers of social and community bonds woven into the very essence of street food.

To immerse ourselves in the rich tapestry of social interactions surrounding street food, ethnographic methods and participant observation serve as our primary tools. Ethnography allows us to step into the lived experiences of individuals, capturing the essence of social engagement in real-time. Through participant observation, the researcher becomes a silent companion at street food stalls, documenting not just what is said but also the non-verbal cues, gestures, and the ambiance that shapes social interactions.

The rationale behind choosing qualitative data collection techniques is rooted in the understanding that street food's social dynamics are nuanced and context-dependent. Qualitative methods provide the depth needed to unravel the intricacies of interpersonal relationships, cultural nuances, and the spontaneous interactions that unfold in the dynamic street food environment. By adopting a qualitative approach, we seek to go beyond mere statistical data, delving into the stories, emotions, and connections that form the social fabric around street food.

Picture a bustling street in Bangalore where the aroma of dosas and the sizzle of frying vadas create a sensory symphony. The researcher, equipped with a notepad and a keen sense of curiosity, becomes an unobtrusive observer at a dosa cart. Through participant observation, the subtle dance of social engagement unfolds—the banter between the vendor and customers, the shared laughter, and the unspoken camaraderie that accompanies each order.

Sampling is a crucial aspect of capturing the diverse social settings within the realm of street food. We employ purposive sampling, carefully selecting participants and locations to ensure a rich and varied representation of social interactions. The criteria for selection encompass geographical diversity, cultural contexts, and variations in vendor-customer dynamics.

Geographical diversity allows us to explore how regional influences shape social engagement, from the street food markets of Delhi to the coastal stalls of Mumbai. Cultural contexts play a pivotal role, with different regions having unique traditions and etiquettes around street food. Variations in vendor-customer dynamics are considered, examining interactions in both established markets and emerging street food scenes.

Every move we make as we explore the social realm of street food is guided by ethical considerations. It is crucial that participants give their informed consent and are aware of the purpose, scope, and goals of the study. Transparency and open communication are upheld over the whole engagement process. Participants are guaranteed the freedom to leave the study at any time without facing repercussions.

Our strategy puts respect for private and cultural sensitivity first. Customers and street food vendors are seen as active participants in the research rather than just subjects. They are appreciated for their views, perspectives, and experiences, and their identities are protected. In order to protect participants from any potential consequences, confidentiality is maintained.

Envision a lively Jaipur night market where the researcher interacts with a group of pals while they savor local cuisine. The researcher joins the conversation with a polite demeanor and an open mind, discovering common experiences, gastronomic tastes, and the cultural relevance of eating on the street.

To sum up, the study design and sampling plan used have been carefully thought out to capture the spirit of social interaction around street food. We seek to reveal the colorful narratives, relationships, and social dynamics that develop in the dynamic fabric of street food environments through anthropological techniques, participant observation, and ethical considerations.

A complex dance between street food vendors and customers takes place in the lively markets and busy lanes where they whack ladles and spatulas. The informal yet deeply meaningful relationships that underpin street food encounters are what make them so vital. In order to shed light on the special rapport and familiarity that add to the overall richness of the street food experience, this section examines the relationships between street food sellers and customers.

Street food vendors frequently play more than just the traditional duties of food purveyors. They develop become listeners, storytellers, and occasionally even confidantes. The casual nature of street food transactions creates an environment conducive to real human interaction. Patrons, both new and returning, find themselves having discussions on topics other than food. Merchants turn the act of buying food into a social gathering by telling stories and recommending their favorite recipes.

The familiarity that exists between street vendors and customers is a major contributing aspect to street food's unique appeal. Frequent patrons experience a sense of community, are frequently greeted by name, and have their preferences remembered. This familiarity not only creates a welcoming atmosphere, but also transforms dining into a shared activity. Street food vendors become community hubs where people congregate and make connections that go beyond commerce.

Imagine a bustling Kolkata street where a pani puri vendor, known as a puchka-wallah, is aware of the desired level of spice for each patron. Mrs. Sen, a frequent customer, enjoys each puchka while regaling others with her day. Street food becomes more than just a sale when the vendor knows her preferences and shows genuine interest in her life. It becomes a treasured ritual of connection.

In addition to offering delectable sensations, street food venues act as distinctive social hubs, promoting inclusivity and dismantling social barriers. This section explores how street food becomes a social equalizer by allowing people from different backgrounds to partake in the culinary mosaic since it is easily accessible and reasonably priced.

Street food markets and stalls defy societal hierarchies, providing a democratic space where individuals from all walks of life converge. Business executives stand alongside construction workers, students mingle with office-goers, and tourists share tables with locals. The act of enjoying a common meal transcends social stratifications, creating an environment where individuals interact as equals, bound by their shared love for street food.

Affordability and accessibility are key factors that contribute to the inclusive nature of street food spaces. Unlike formal dining establishments that may carry certain economic connotations, street food is often budget-friendly. The modest prices make it accessible to a broad spectrum of society, encouraging diverse social interactions. A street food stall becomes a microcosm of societal diversity, where economic backgrounds fade into the background, and the focus shifts to the shared pleasure of a good meal.

Imagine a vibrant street food market in Mumbai, where a group of college students eagerly gathers around a vada pav stall. The affordability of the snack ensures that economic differences dissolve as students from various backgrounds bond over their shared delight in the spicy, flavorful bites. The street food stall becomes a great equalizer, where the enjoyment of affordable, delicious food fosters connections among individuals who might not otherwise cross paths.

With its wide range of tastes, street food is more than just a gourmet adventure—it promotes cross-cultural dialogue and integration. This section looks at case studies that show how street food can be used to promote appreciation and understanding across cultural boundaries.

Street food, by its very nature, encapsulates the essence of different cultures. Vendors often bring with them not just recipes but also the traditions, stories, and cultural nuances of their regions. This diversity transforms street food spaces into arenas for cultural exchange. Customers, in exploring unfamiliar dishes, engage in a sensory journey that goes beyond taste, encompassing the rich cultural tapestry from which the food originates.

Street food spaces provide a stage for cultural integration, where individuals from varied backgrounds converge to appreciate and celebrate each other's culinary traditions. This integration is not just about the food itself but extends to the interactions between vendors and customers. Through the act of ordering, sharing, and enjoying street food, individuals partake in a form of cultural diplomacy, fostering connections that bridge cultural gaps.

Visualize a street food festival in Chennai, where a dosa vendor from Karnataka shares his traditional masala dosa with locals. As customers savor the flavors, conversations emerge about the cultural nuances of the dish, its significance, and the regional variations. The street food cart becomes a miniature embassy of cultural exchange, where understanding and appreciation blossom over shared meals.

With their rainbow of tastes, street food festivals have developed into more than just gastronomic events. These are lively gatherings that bind communities together by fostering common interests and strengthening the links that keep neighborhoods alive. This section addresses the significance of community-led street food projects in promoting local culture, as well as the effects of street food festivals as community activities.

Street food festivals are more than simply culinary extravaganzas; they are memorable events that foster community. This section looks at how these events, with their wide range of food options, act as catalysts to promote community harmony. The social aspect of eating street food fits in well with the festival environment, fostering an environment where locals gather to celebrate what makes their community unique.

Street food festivals are lively exhibitions of regional skill that highlight the variety of cuisine customs that exist within a community. These gatherings have an effect on locals' pride and sense of identity, which goes beyond just enjoying meals in the moment. Examining the socio-cultural importance of street food festivals reveals their capacity to strengthen ties among communities and leave enduring impressions.

Collaborative experiences are fundamental to the unity of a community. Street food festivals offer a platform for locals to experience the excitement of exploration through their lively booths, on-site acts, and hands-on cooking classes. Trying out different foods, talking to merchants, and taking part in group activities all contribute to a feeling of community. These celebrations contribute to the collective identity of the community by acting as a live repository of shared memories.

Imagine a bustling street food festival in Jaipur, where families assemble to enjoy a range of regional specialties under vibrant tents. Together, the sounds of laughter and live music blend with the perfume of spices as inhabitants weave together a tapestry of common experiences. In addition to tantalizing the senses, the festival serves as a platform for creating enduring relationships within the neighborhood.

Communities frequently take the initiative to stage their own street food events in addition to official festivals. This section looks at situations when locals plan street food events to support their community's culture. These programs demonstrate a grassroots strategy for fostering a sense of community as locals take charge of the story and highlight the distinctive characteristics that make their area special.

Community-led street food initiatives vary widely in scale and nature. From neighborhood potlucks to monthly food markets organized by residents, these initiatives contribute to the rich tapestry of local culture. Exploring such instances unveils the organic nature of these events and the genuine passion residents invest in preserving and promoting their culinary heritage.

The cooperation of vendors and locals is typically the key to the success of community-led street food programs. These activities are greatly aided by the participation of local vendors, who are essential members of the community. This partnership transcends transactional exchanges and instead becomes a joint enterprise in which vendors actively contribute to building the community's culinary story.

Local vendors are empowered by collaborative projects, which provide them a stage on which to demonstrate their abilities and establish a more personal connection with locals. Residents and sellers develop a mutually beneficial cooperation that strengthens the feeling of communal control over the food scene.

Imagine a neighborhood in Bangalore setting up a street food bazaar every month at a nearby park. Local vendors and residents work together to develop a meal that showcases the region's unique culinary heritage. In addition to uniting the community, the program makes vendors who participate in the celebration of their regional delicacies feel proud of what they do.

As we conclude this flavorful exploration into the social and community aspects of street food, it is essential to recapitulate the key findings that have emerged from the rich tapestry of our research. Street food, beyond being a culinary delight, is a dynamic force that weaves together the intricate threads of social interactions, community bonds, and cultural celebrations.

Our investigation into the anthropology of street food has shown us that these modest stands and carts serve as more than just food vendors; they are also cultural icons that unite

local communities. The interactions that developed between suppliers and consumers were casual yet meaningful, encouraging familiarity and a sense of community. Street food has become a social equalizer, dismantling boundaries and fostering inclusive cultures because of its accessibility and cost.

Whether they were organized or community-driven, street food festivals were revealed to be more than just gastronomic events. They act as lively exhibitions of regional talent, fostering experiences that are shared and strengthen the sense of community. The symbiotic relationship between street food and community life is further reinforced by collaborative initiatives between vendors and citizens at these events.

The implications of our findings extend far beyond the immediate realms of taste and aroma. Street food, embedded in the urban landscape, plays a pivotal role in enhancing the quality of urban life. It creates spaces for genuine social engagement, breaking the monotony of daily routines. Affordability and accessibility make street food a common ground where diverse populations converge, fostering a sense of unity and shared experiences. Street food becomes not just a culinary choice but a lifestyle that nourishes communities beyond their palates.

In brief, street food has a social power that transcends the boundaries of carts and stalls and nourishes communities in ways that go beyond taste buds. More lively, inclusive, and connected urban neighborhoods can be created if we acknowledge, embrace, and actively utilize the social potential of street food. As we move forward, let's take a trip where the sound of street food pans sizzling combines to create a symphony of human experiences that intertwines the various strands that make up urban life.

Section 8

STREET FOOD AND ENTREPRENEURSHIP

In this section, we revisit the journey through the flavorful landscape of street food, exploring the symbiotic relationship between street food and entrepreneurship in the vibrant context of India. From the bustling markets of Delhi to the coastal stalls of Mumbai, street food vendors embody the spirit of entrepreneurship, turning roadside carts into thriving businesses. Let's recapitulate the key findings that illuminate the entrepreneurial spice within the tapestry of street food.

In addition to being delicious, street food is a microcosm of entrepreneurship. The sellers exhibit incredible tenacity and inventiveness despite frequently having little funding. They exhibit the entrepreneurial spirit that drives their endeavors forward as they maneuver through the complex network of licenses, permits, and rules. Street food vendors are the epitome of entrepreneurial agility; they not only deliberately select good locations but also alter recipes to suit local tastes.

The economic impact of street food entrepreneurship is substantial, contributing not only to the livelihoods of individual vendors but also to the broader economy. Street food clusters become economic hubs, attracting footfall and fostering ancillary businesses. The economic significance extends beyond the immediate transactional exchanges, creating a ripple effect that influences local markets and stimulates economic activities.

India's street food vendors, who transform humble carts into thriving food businesses, are the epitome of entrepreneurship. Past the sound of pans frying and spices frying, these vendors exhibit outstanding qualities of entrepreneurship. Their ability to bounce back from setbacks in the ever-changing street food market is a trademark. They are risk-takers who work in the unorganized sector and enter the uncharted territory of street vending with grit and resourcefulness.

One of the key characteristics of street food entrepreneurship is adaptability. Vendors modify their products frequently to suit regional inclinations. Their inventiveness and flexibility in adapting to shifting market conditions are examples of their entrepreneurial agility. Street food vendors are at the vanguard of culinary innovation, whether they're creating fusion flavors that pique customers' interest or giving a classic recipe a distinctive touch.

Making skillful use of regional ingredients is one of the distinguishing features of street food business in India. Vendors turn basic materials into culinary creations, frequently purchasing products from local marketplaces. Street food sellers display their culinary prowess and business acumen as they provide everything from the classic vada pav to speciality dishes like dosa and puchka from their own regions.

There is a strong link between street food entrepreneurship and regional ecosystems. Because they are aware of the needs of their neighborhood, vendors include locally grown produce and flavors in their products. This develops a feeling of communal pride in addition to forging a unique culinary identity. Street food vendors serve as the keepers of regional culinary traditions, turning their stands into hubs of flavor.

Street food vendors must use entrepreneurial innovation to overcome regulatory obstacles while operating in the unregulated sector. They successfully negotiate bureaucratic obstacles by being resilient and using innovative problem- solving to get licenses and follow sanitary regulations. Their capacity for regulatory compliance while maintaining the seamless functioning of their firms is evidence of their prowess as entrepreneurs.

Street food vendors frequently create unofficial networks to exchange knowledge and approaches to overcoming legal obstacles. Working together within these networks not only keeps vendors updated on regulatory developments, but it also establishes a support network where manufacturers may pool their resources to address shared problems. The entrepreneurial spirit of the community is apparent as vendors collaborate to discover creative ways to handle the regulatory environment.

Street food vendors' entrepreneurial journeys have changed throughout time. Many vendors have embraced social media and internet platforms because they understand how important it is to have a digital presence and to reach a wider audience. Street food vendors are utilizing technology to grow their enterprises, from visually appealing food photos that entice online shoppers to online ordering platforms that satisfy the needs of contemporary consumers.

This change demonstrates both their agility and their business vision. Previously operating just out of carts on street corners, vendors now have virtual storefronts that are not limited by location. Along with increasing business visibility, the digital

leap creates new opportunities for customer interaction. Not only are street food sellers business owners, but they also represent the culinary arts by using digital platforms to tell their stories and connect with a global audience.

street food vendors in India exemplify the spirit of entrepreneurship. With resilience, adaptability, and creative problem-solving, they navigate the complex landscape of street food. Transforming local ingredients into culinary delights, they contribute not only to the gastronomic landscape but also to the cultural identity of their communities. From carts to digital platforms, they embrace technological advancements, evolving into ambassadors of culinary innovation in the vibrant tapestry of street food entrepreneurship.

Adaptability is a defining feature of street food entrepreneurship. Vendors constantly adjust their offerings to meet local tastes and preferences. The ability to innovate and pivot in response to changing market demands is a testament to their entrepreneurial agility. Whether it's introducing a unique twist to a traditional recipe or crafting fusion flavors that capture the imagination of customers, street food vendors are at the forefront of culinary innovation.

Making skillful use of regional ingredients is one of the distinguishing features of street food business in India. Vendors turn basic materials into culinary creations, frequently purchasing products from local marketplaces. Street food sellers display their culinary prowess and business acumen as they provide everything from the classic vada pav to speciality dishes like dosa and puchka from their own regions.

There is a strong link between street food entrepreneurship and regional ecosystems. Because they are aware of the needs of their neighborhood, vendors include locally grown produce and flavors in their products. This develops a feeling of communal pride in addition to forging a unique culinary identity. Street food vendors serve as the keepers of regional culinary traditions, turning their stands into hubs of flavor.

The entrepreneurial journey of street food vendors has witnessed a digital transformation, emphasizing their adaptability to modern trends. Recognizing the importance of a digital presence, many vendors have embraced online platforms and social media to extend their reach. Instagram-worthy food posts, online menus, and delivery services have become integral parts of their entrepreneurial toolkit.

This shift is not just about reaching a wider audience; it's about storytelling. Street food vendors are no longer confined to physical carts on street corners; they have become ambassadors of culinary experiences in the virtual world. Through digital platforms, they share the stories behind their dishes, connect with customers on a personal level, and showcase the richness of India's street food culture to a global audience.

Let's look at a story of a vendor in Kanpur.

Thakur Prasad Gupta: A Chaat Maestro Blending Tradition and Entrepreneurship

In the heart of Kanpur, where the bustling streets come alive with the aroma of spices and the sizzle of street food, there resides a chaat stall that holds a special place in the culinary tapestry of the city. Meet Thakur Prasad Gupta, the man behind Mayuri Chaat, where flavors dance and stories unfold.

Thakur Prasad's journey from joblessness to becoming a chaat maestro is a tale of resilience and entrepreneurial vision. In the early '90s, when life dealt him the cards of unemployment, destiny took him on a journey to Gwalior. During this expedition, he stumbled upon a hotel named Mayuri, a name that left an indelible mark on his mind. Enchanted by the allure of the name, he made a silent pact with himself that whenever he ventured into his own business, it would bear the same moniker.

In 1992, Thakur Prasad found himself in the bustling lanes of Kanpur, armed with a dream and the essence of Mayuri in his heart. With unwavering determination, he set up his own chaat stall, and thus, Mayuri Chaat was born. The stall, tucked in a corner, soon became a beacon for chaat enthusiasts seeking an extraordinary experience.

What sets Mayuri Chaat apart is not just the delectable array of chaat delicacies but the unique touch of Thakur Prasad's vision. His specialty lies in the use of ayurvedic masalas, a secret blend of spices passed down through generations. Each bite tells a story of tradition, carefully crafted by the hands of a man who believes in the holistic essence of his culinary creations.

The chaat stall quickly became a haven for locals and visitors alike. Thakur Prasad's commitment to quality and authenticity resonates in every plate he serves. From the iconic aloo tikki to the tangy pani puri, Mayuri Chaat is a symphony of flavors that captivates the senses.

Thakur Prasad Gupta's entrepreneurial spirit is not just about running a successful chaat stall; it's about embracing heritage and infusing it into every aspect of his business. The name Mayuri, once a source of inspiration, now stands tall as a symbol of his dedication to excellence.

As patrons gather around Mayuri Chaat, they aren't just relishing chaat; they are partaking in a legacy crafted with love, determination, and a sprinkle of ayurvedic magic. Thakur Prasad's story is a testament to the fact that entrepreneurship is not merely a profession; it's a canvas where dreams and traditions come together to create something truly extraordinary. In the heart of Kanpur, Mayuri Chaat stands as a living testament to Thakur Prasad Gupta's journey – a journey that turned a humble chaat stall into a culinary institution, enriching the streets of Kanpur with the flavors of tradition and entrepreneurship.

The essence of street food extends far beyond the mere transaction of food; it encompasses a micro-entrepreneurship ecosystem that nurtures local economies. Street food vendors, often operating with minimal resources, become the backbone of this ecosystem. Their businesses create a ripple effect, influencing not only their livelihoods but also the broader economic landscape.

In local markets and bustling street corners, street food vendors set up shop, contributing to the vibrancy of these spaces. The economic impact goes beyond the immediate sale of food; it stimulates ancillary businesses, such as local suppliers of ingredients, cart manufacturers, and even waste management services. The interconnected web of micro- entrepreneurship creates a thriving local economy, where each participant plays a vital role in the ecosystem.

Street food has a great role in empowering women entrepreneurs, which makes it a remarkable stimulant for micro-entrepreneurship. The profession of selling street food has historically been dominated by men in many cultures. But something is changing—more and more women are stepping out into the street food industry as entrepreneurs.

Women entrepreneurs are shattering stereotypes by starting up shops, providing a variety of gastronomic treats, and improving the local economy. Beyond just having an economic impact, this empowerment questions social conventions and promotes an atmosphere that is more varied and inclusive for entrepreneurs. Women can use street food as a platform to demonstrate their culinary prowess, achieve financial independence, and dispel stereotypes about gender roles in entrepreneurship.

The social impact of street food as a catalyst for micro-entrepreneurship is profound, particularly in the context of local communities. Street food vendors, often deeply embedded in the social fabric of their neighborhoods, become not just food providers but pillars of community pride and resilience.

The presence of vibrant street food stalls creates communal spaces where residents gather, interact, and forge connections. These spaces become hubs for social interactions, fostering a sense of belonging and shared pride among community members. The pride extends beyond individual vendors; it encompasses the community's identity and its culinary heritage, creating a tapestry of shared experiences.

In times of adversity, such as economic downturns or crises, street food vendors often display remarkable resilience. The micro-entrepreneurship ecosystem, built on relationships and shared experiences, acts as a buffer, helping communities withstand challenges. Street food becomes more than a source of income; it becomes a symbol of community strength and resilience.

Case Study: Maya's Spice Corner - Empowering Women in Street Food

Maya, a resilient woman from a local community, decided to break the mold and set up Maya's Spice Corner, a street food stall known for its flavorful snacks. Maya's journey into street food entrepreneurship not only transformed her life but also became an inspiration for other women in her community.

Maya's Spice Corner, nestled in a vibrant corner of the local market, serves a variety of snacks infused with authentic spices. Maya's commitment to quality and her entrepreneurial spirit have turned her stall into a local favorite. What sets Maya apart is not just the culinary expertise she brings to her dishes but also her role as a trailblazer for women entrepreneurs.

Maya's success has sparked a positive change in her community. Other women have been inspired to explore their culinary talents and set up their own stalls. The local market, once dominated by male vendors, now boasts a more diverse and inclusive array of street food options. Maya's Spice Corner has become a symbol of empowerment, demonstrating how street food can break gender barriers and empower women to become successful micro-entrepreneurs.

As we explore the catalytic role of street food in micro-entrepreneurship, it becomes evident that its potential is far from exhausted. Looking ahead, there is an opportunity to leverage this vibrant ecosystem for sustainable and inclusive economic growth.

Stakeholders, including local governments and non-governmental organizations, can play a crucial role in providing support structures for street food vendors. Access to training programs, financial resources, and mentorship opportunities can empower vendors to enhance their entrepreneurial skills and navigate regulatory challenges more effectively.

Additionally, initiatives that celebrate and preserve local culinary traditions can further enrich the micro-entrepreneurship landscape. Street food festivals, community-led events, and collaborations with local culinary schools can create platforms for vendors to showcase their unique offerings, attracting a broader audience and contributing to the cultural richness of communities.

Street food, with its rich flavors and enticing fragrances, is more than just a tasty cuisine; it's a powerful force behind microbusiness. The influence of street food on local economies is immense, ranging from empowering women entrepreneurs to building communal resilience. As we look to the future, let's acknowledge the promise of street food as a driver of inclusive, sustainable economic growth, where each bite and taste serves as a foundation for strong, dynamic communities.

To nurture the entrepreneurial spirit within the street food landscape, there is an imperative need for strengthened support structures. Local governments, in collaboration with non-governmental organizations, can play a pivotal role in providing avenues for street food entrepreneurs to enhance their skills, access financial resources, and receive mentorship.

Training Programs:

Initiatives that offer training programs in food safety, business management, and culinary innovation can equip street food vendors with the skills needed to thrive in a competitive market. These programs can be tailored to address the specific needs of street food entrepreneurs, covering topics such as regulatory compliance, customer service, and sustainable practices.

Financial Resources:

Access to financial resources is a critical factor in the sustainability and growth of street food businesses. Governments can establish micro-financing schemes or grants specifically designed for street food entrepreneurs. These financial resources can be utilized for equipment upgrades, expansion, and adapting to emerging market trends.

Mentorship Opportunities:

Establishing mentorship programs where experienced street food vendors guide newcomers can facilitate knowledge transfer and foster a sense of community within the industry. Mentorship can provide valuable insights into navigating regulatory challenges, managing finances, and sustaining a successful street food business.

Technology offers street food entrepreneurs both benefits and challenges in this era of digital revolution. Accepting these technical developments might lead to new opportunities in terms of business expansion, marketing, and consumer interaction.

Online Platforms:

Creating user-friendly online platforms for street food vendors can enhance their visibility and reach a broader customer base. Mobile apps that provide information about vendors, their specialties, and user reviews can make street food more accessible to tech-savvy consumers.

Digital Payments:

Facilitating digital payment options at street food stalls can enhance convenience for customers and streamline transactions for vendors. Governments can collaborate with financial institutions to promote the adoption of digital payment methods among street food entrepreneurs.

Social Media Marketing:

Leveraging social media platforms for marketing and promotion can be a game-changer for street food vendors. Training programs that teach vendors how to effectively use platforms like Instagram, Facebook, and Twitter can enhance their marketing strategies and attract a younger, tech-savvy audience.

In crafting policies for the future of street food, it is essential to recognize and embrace the diversity inherent in the industry. Inclusive policies that consider the unique challenges and opportunities of different vendors can ensure equitable growth.

Policy Flexibility:

Governments can develop policies that are flexible and adaptable to the diverse needs of street food vendors. Recognizing the different scales of operation, from individual carts to larger food clusters, ensures that regulations are reasonable and conducive to the varied nature of street food businesses.

Support for Marginalized Groups:

Policies can be designed to provide targeted support for marginalized groups entering the street food industry. This may include women entrepreneurs, minority communities, or individuals with limited resources. Financial incentives, training programs, and mentorship opportunities can facilitate the inclusion of diverse voices in the street food landscape.

Community Engagement:

Inclusive policies should involve community stakeholders, including street food vendors, in decision-making processes. Creating avenues for dialogue and feedback ensures that policies are reflective of the needs and aspirations of the diverse street food community.

In conclusion, the future of street food is teeming with possibilities, but realizing its full potential requires strategic planning and supportive policies. Strengthening support structures, embracing technological advancements, preserving culinary traditions, promoting sustainability, and crafting inclusive policies are key elements in nurturing the sizzle of street food. As we move forward, let us envision a street food landscape where entrepreneurship thrives, cultural heritage is celebrated, and communities are empowered through the flavors that define them.

Section 9
STREET FOOD AND GLOBALIZATION

Street food, a ubiquitous and flavorful facet of culinary traditions worldwide, has a rich history deeply intertwined with the cultural tapestry of nations. The roots of street food can be traced back to ancient civilizations, where bustling marketplaces and vibrant streets served as hubs for culinary exploration. In ancient Rome, for example, popinae (similar to today's food stalls) dotted the city streets, offering a diverse range of snacks and meals for the urban population.

Moving forward through history, the Silk Road played a pivotal role in the exchange of goods, ideas, and, of course, culinary delights. Street food became a symbol of cultural exchange, as traders and travelers brought their gastronomic treasures to new lands, influencing local cuisines and leaving an indelible mark on the culinary map.

In more recent times, the Industrial Revolution and urbanization further fueled the rise of street food. As people migrated to cities in search of work, street vendors became an essential part of the urban landscape, offering quick and affordable sustenance to a growing population.

Simultaneously, street food became a vibrant expression of cultural diversity, reflecting the amalgamation of various culinary traditions within burgeoning metropolises.

The globalization of street food is a phenomenon that transcends geographical boundaries, creating a dynamic interplay between local and global influences. This study seeks to unravel the intricacies of this interplay within the Indian context, a nation renowned for its diverse and flavorful street food culture.

As India stands at the crossroads of tradition and modernity, its street food landscape provides a fascinating lens through which to examine the impact of globalization. The study aims to delve into how international flavors, culinary techniques, and cultural exchanges have shaped and redefined India's vibrant street food scene.

By understanding the globalization dynamics at play, this research seeks to shed light on how Indian street food vendors navigate the delicate balance between preserving cultural authenticity and embracing global influences. It aims to explore how the infusion of international elements has enhanced or altered traditional Indian street food, offering a nuanced perspective on the evolving tastes and preferences of a diverse population.

The scope of this study extends beyond the mere examination of recipes and ingredients. It encompasses a holistic exploration of the cultural implications of globalized street food in India. From the bustling streets of Delhi with its spicy chaats to the vibrant markets of Mumbai adorned with vada pavs, this research aims to traverse the length and breadth of India, capturing the essence of how globalization has permeated its diverse street food offerings.

The significance of this study lies in its potential to contribute to a broader discourse on cultural identity and globalization. India, with its myriad regional cuisines, presents a unique case study for understanding how globalization influences not just the flavors on the plate but also the cultural narratives embedded in each bite. By unraveling these complexities, the research seeks to offer insights that extend beyond the culinary realm, providing a nuanced understanding of the broader socio-cultural impacts of globalization on a nation's street food heritage.

In the following sections, we will embark on a flavorful journey through the bustling streets of India, exploring the crossroads where tradition and globalization converge to shape the nation's dynamic street food culture.

Globalisation, a term that resonates across various disciplines, encompasses economic, cultural, and social dimensions, weaving together a complex tapestry that spans continents and transcends borders. In the economic realm, globalization refers to the increasing interconnectedness of markets and the flow of goods, capital, and services across nations. Culturally, it signifies the exchange and diffusion of ideas, values, and traditions, while socially, it involves the interconnectedness of people and communities on a global scale.

Within the Indian context, globalization is palpable in the economic surge, cultural amalgamation, and social transformations that have unfolded over the past few decades. The liberalization of the Indian economy in the

1990s opened doors to foreign investments, trade, and collaborations, fostering an environment where global influences permeated various aspects of Indian society, including its vibrant culinary landscape.

The impact of globalization on culinary practices is profound, reshaping not only what ends up on the plate but also how it is sourced, prepared, and consumed. In India, a nation with a deeply rooted culinary heritage, globalization has led to a confluence of traditional and international elements.

One noticeable change is the shift in food consumption patterns. As urbanization accelerates and lifestyles evolve, there is a growing demand for convenience and variety. Fast food chains, influenced by Western culinary traditions, have become ubiquitous in Indian cities. This shift is not just about the type of food but also the way it is consumed— quick, on- the-go, and often reflective of global trends.

Moreover, globalization has facilitated the availability of diverse ingredients from around the world, enabling chefs and home cooks alike to experiment with new flavors and techniques. This fusion of global and local ingredients has given rise to innovative culinary creations, bridging the gap between traditional Indian dishes and international cuisines.

In the bustling streets of India, where the vibrancy of culture meets the fervor of commerce, the emergence of a global street food culture is palpable. Street food, once emblematic of local flavors and regional specialties, has become a canvas for cultural interconnectedness in the era of globalization.

Indian street food vendors, traditionally known for serving local delights, now incorporate international elements into their offerings. The iconic vada pav may share space with a Mexican-inspired corn on the cob, and the ubiquitous chaat may be infused with Mediterranean flavors. These culinary mash-ups not only cater to evolving taste preferences but also symbolize the intermingling of global influences with India's rich gastronomic heritage.

Street food, in this context, serves as more than just a source of sustenance—it becomes a tangible representation of the global village. The street corners adorned with diverse food carts are microcosms of cultural exchange, where vendors adapt their offerings to cater to an increasingly cosmopolitan palate. This culinary fusion not only reflects the globalized tastes of consumers but also celebrates the diversity of the nation's street food scene.

Moreover, the emergence of global street food culture goes beyond the mere introduction of international flavors. It embodies a spirit of openness and acceptance, fostering a sense of shared culinary experiences among people from different walks of life. The street, once a local culinary arena, is now a stage where the world converges, and cultural narratives unfold in the sizzling pans and aromatic spices of street vendors.

In the subsequent sections of this exploration, we will delve deeper into specific instances and examples of how globalization has shaped the intricate tapestry of street food in India, examining the fusion of flavors, the evolution of recipes, and the cultural dialogues playing out in the heart of bustling markets and busy streets.

Embarking on a culinary journey across the globe, we encounter a myriad of street food delights that have transcended borders, becoming beloved in unexpected corners of the world. These case studies exemplify the power of international flavor adoption, transforming local street food scenes into melting pots of global gastronomy.

In the vibrant streets of Tokyo, where tradition meets modernity, the scent of sizzling tacos wafts through the air. Japanese food stalls have embraced the Mexican marvel, infusing their own unique twists. Imagine a bustling street corner where savory miso-marinated beef fills soft taco shells, adorned with a sprinkle of shichimi togarashi for an extra kick. The fusion of Japanese umami and Mexican zest creates a taco experience unlike any other, captivating locals and tourists alike.

The iconic Vietnamese banh mi has found a second home on the streets of Paris, exemplifying the cross-cultural pollination of flavors. French baguettes serve as the vessel for succulent grilled meats, pickled vegetables, and a smear of pâté. What started as a culinary dialogue between Vietnam and France has evolved into a global sensation, with banh mi vendors in Paris crafting sandwiches that pay homage to both Vietnamese tradition and French sophistication.

In the bustling markets of Mexico City, the familiar aroma of shawarma mingles with the scents of local spices. Mexican street food vendors have embraced the Middle Eastern delight, creating a fusion that reflects the cultural diversity of the city. Picture thinly sliced al pastor-style marinated meat, rotating on a vertical spit, served in a tortilla with a medley of fresh salsa and avocado. The marriage of Middle Eastern technique and Mexican flair creates a street food sensation that transcends culinary borders.

In the heart of Mumbai, where the bustling streets are alive with the rhythm of life, a small food cart tells a story of culinary cross-pollination. Meet Raj, a third-generation street food vendor, whose humble stall has become a microcosm of global flavors.

Raj's grandfather started the business with a singular focus on traditional Indian street food. However, as globalization seeped into the culinary landscape, Raj found himself drawn to the idea of infusing international flavors into his family's recipes.

One day, inspired by the aromas of a nearby Thai food truck, Raj decided to experiment. He introduced a fusion dish that combined the vibrant flavors of Thai green curry with the comforting warmth of Indian masalas. The result? A fragrant, flavorful curry served over a bed of steaming rice, garnished with cilantro and lime. Word quickly spread through the bustling neighborhood, and Raj's Thai-Indian fusion dish became a sensation. Locals, tourists, and even international food bloggers flocked to Raj's cart, drawn by the allure of this unexpected culinary marriage.

Soon, other vendors in the area took notice. The aroma of global spices began to fill the air as neighboring stalls experimented with their own fusion creations. Italian-inspired dosas, Japanese-infused chaat, and Korean-spiced samosas—all crafted with a local touch—transformed the once- traditional street into a haven of culinary innovation.

Raj's story is just one of many echoing through the winding lanes of street food culture. Culinary cross-pollination, driven by a spirit of experimentation and openness, has transformed local street food scenes into vibrant hubs where the world converges on a plate.

As we explore further, it becomes evident that the adoption of international flavors is not just about changing recipes; it's about fostering a sense of curiosity, creativity, and cultural exchange that breathes new life into the age-old tradition of street food. The next sections will delve into the broader implications of this cross-cultural culinary dance, examining how it shapes identity, fosters understanding, and celebrates the diversity of global street food.

Fusion cuisine, a term that has sparked both excitement and debate in culinary circles, finds a vibrant home on the bustling streets of India. At its core, fusion cuisine involves the artful blending of culinary traditions, marrying flavors, techniques, and ingredients from disparate cultures to create something entirely new and often unexpected. On the streets, where vendors become culinary alchemists, fusion cuisine becomes a dynamic expression of creativity and adaptation.

In the Indian context, fusion cuisine on the streets is a testament to the nation's rich tapestry of culinary traditions. Street food vendors, inspired by global flavors and local ingredients, embark on a journey of experimentation, weaving together a culinary kaleidoscope that reflects the cultural diversity of the streets.

In the labyrinthine lanes of Mumbai, where the aroma of spices dances in the air, a street vendor named Ananya concocted a fusion masterpiece — the Pizza Dosa.

Ananya skillfully combines the crispiness of the South Indian dosa with the savory allure of Italian pizza. Picture a dosa adorned with tomato sauce, melted cheese, and an array of toppings, transforming a humble South Indian staple into a global sensation that captivates locals and tourists alike.

In the heart of Delhi, where chaat reigns supreme, a visionary street food vendor named Ravi introduced a fusion dish that transcends borders — Sushi Chaat. Drawing inspiration from Japanese sushi and the vibrant flavors of Indian chaat, Ravi crafts bite-sized sushi rolls bursting with the tanginess of tamarind chutney and the crunch of sev. This delightful marriage of East and West, tradition and innovation, has become a symbol of Delhi's cosmopolitan street food scene.

Bangalore, a city known for its tech hubs and diverse culinary landscape, boasts a fusion creation that marries the fiery flavors of Korea with the beloved Indian street food, Vada Pav. Street vendor Deepak's Kimchi Vada Pav features a spicy kimchi-infused potato patty sandwiched between soft pav buns, creating a harmonious blend of Korean and Indian culinary elements. The dish has become a sensation, attracting locals and adventurous food enthusiasts eager to experience this spicy cross-cultural delight.

While fusion cuisine on the streets presents a tantalizing array of flavors, it also navigates the delicate balance between authenticity and innovation. In the Indian context, where culinary traditions are deeply rooted and diverse, street food vendors face both challenges and opportunities in their quest to create fusion masterpieces.

One challenge lies in navigating cultural sensitivities. Street vendors must be mindful of the origins and significance of the culinary traditions they fuse. The key is to approach fusion with respect, and understanding the cultural context of each ingredient and technique. For example, when blending Indian and Mexican flavors, it is crucial to honor the essence of both cuisines, avoiding cultural appropriation and fostering a genuine celebration of diversity.

Another challenge is the constant tightrope walk between authenticity and innovation. While the fusion of global and local elements is celebrated, there is a risk of diluting the authenticity of traditional dishes. Street food vendors must strike a delicate balance, ensuring that the fusion enhances rather than overwhelms the original flavors. This requires a deep understanding of the cultural roots of each dish and a commitment to preserving its essence while introducing innovative twists.

Amidst these challenges, fusion cuisine on the streets of India presents a myriad of opportunities. The dynamic nature of street food allows for unparalleled creativity and experimentation. Vendors have the freedom to play with flavors, reinvent classics, and introduce dishes that challenge traditional norms. This not only attracts a diverse customer base but also positions street food as a vibrant symbol of cultural evolution and openness to culinary exploration.

In the subsequent sections, we will delve deeper into the stories behind these fusion creations, exploring the narratives of the street vendors who dare to blend traditions and challenge culinary norms. Through their stories, we uncover the passion, innovation, and cultural sensitivity that define the landscape of fusion cuisine on the bustling streets of India.

On the bustling streets of India, where the tapestry of cultures is woven into every dish, street food emerges not only as a source of sustenance but as a cultural ambassador fostering dialogue and understanding between diverse communities. The hawkers and vendors become inadvertent diplomats, using the language of flavors to bridge cultural gaps and create a shared culinary experience.

India, with its rich cultural heritage and diverse regional cuisines, offers a fascinating canvas for this culinary diplomacy. Street food, in particular, serves as an accessible and inclusive medium for cultural exchange, transcending language barriers and fostering a sense of shared humanity.

Imagine a street corner in Delhi where a vendor skillfully crafts falafel wraps, engaging with customers from different backgrounds. As the scent of Middle Eastern spices mingles with the vibrancy of Indian masalas, conversations flow, and cultural boundaries blur. In this way, street food becomes a vehicle for dialogue, breaking down preconceived notions and building connections one bite at a time.

The globalization of street food leaves an indelible imprint on local culinary identity and tradition. In the

Indian context, where food is deeply intertwined with cultural and regional identity, the influx of international flavors reshapes the narrative of traditional dishes.

Street food vendors, once stewards of time-honored recipes, now find themselves navigating the delicate balance between preserving cultural authenticity and embracing global influences. Traditional dishes undergo a metamorphosis, adapting to contemporary tastes and reflecting the changing culinary landscape.

For instance, the ubiquitous chaat, a quintessential Indian street food, has evolved to incorporate diverse international elements. Aloo tikkis may now be crowned with avocado salsa, and tamarind chutney might mingle with soy sauce. While this evolution introduces exciting flavors and attracts a broader audience, it also prompts questions about the preservation of culinary heritage.

However, the impact is not solely transformative; it is also generative. Globalization sparks creativity among street food vendors, inspiring them to experiment with new ingredients and techniques while staying rooted in tradition. This synthesis of old and new becomes a dynamic expression of culinary identity, reflecting the ongoing dialogue between tradition and innovation.

As street food becomes a conduit for cultural exchange, a nuanced challenge arises: the fine line between appreciation and appropriation. Cultural appropriation occurs when elements of one culture are adopted by another, often without proper understanding or respect for the cultural context. In the Indian street food scene, this challenge is palpable as vendors navigate the complexities of integrating international flavors while preserving the integrity of their culinary roots.

Street food vendors must tread carefully, ensuring that their creations are born out of respect rather than exploitation. A fusion dish that pays homage to another culture with appreciation for its nuances fosters cultural understanding. However, when elements are borrowed without understanding or presented out of context, it can lead to misrepresentation and perpetuate stereotypes.

Maintaining authenticity is paramount in navigating the fine line of cultural exchange. Street food vendors must be attuned to the cultural sensitivities associated with the ingredients they use and the manner in which they present them. This requires a commitment to learning about the origins and significance of each component and incorporating them with due respect.

To address the challenges of cultural appropriation, collaboration and education become essential tools. Collaborative efforts between vendors from different cultural backgrounds can lead to a richer exchange of ideas and a more nuanced understanding of each other's culinary traditions. Additionally, educating both vendors and consumers about the cultural context of specific dishes fosters a climate of appreciation rather than appropriation.

In the following sections, we will explore real-life stories from street food vendors in India who navigate these challenges and triumph in their quest to create a culinary landscape that is both globally influenced and locally rooted. Through their experiences, we gain insights into the transformative power of street food as a cultural ambassador and the delicate dance of preserving identity in the face of globalization.

The vibrant streets of India echo not only with the sizzling sounds of street food but also with the entrepreneurial spirit of those who turn humble food carts into thriving businesses. Street food, beyond being a culinary delight, serves as a gateway for small-scale entrepreneurs to realize their dreams, providing economic opportunities that ripple through local communities.

In India, where the informal sector is a significant contributor to the economy, street food becomes a symbol of grassroots entrepreneurship. Vendors, often starting with modest setups and family recipes, carve out niches in bustling markets, creating livelihoods that extend beyond their individual enterprises.

In the heart of Jaipur, Kavita, a determined entrepreneur, set up her chaat cart with a recipe passed down through generations. What started as a small venture on the pavement became a local sensation. Kavita's chaat cart not only served delectable snacks but also became a community hub. As her business grew, Kavita employed local help, contributing not just to her family's income but also to the economic vibrancy of the neighborhood.

Street food entrepreneurship thrives on simplicity and accessibility. The initial investment is often modest, making it an accessible avenue for individuals with limited resources to enter the business world. It fosters self-employment, empowering entrepreneurs to shape their destinies while adding flavors to the local economy.

While globalization has undeniably expanded the horizons of street food, bringing new flavors and culinary influences, it also plays a pivotal role in shaping the economic landscape of street food economies in India.

Globalization transforms the street food cart from a local venture into a participant in a global culinary marketplace. Vendors have the opportunity to experiment with international flavors, attracting a diverse customer base that includes locals and tourists alike. The exposure to global tastes not only broadens the culinary horizons of consumers but also translates into economic gains for street food entrepreneurs.

Additionally, the rise of social media and food tourism has further amplified the economic impact. A well-photographed dish can become a viral sensation, drawing in food enthusiasts from different corners of the world. Street food vendors, armed with unique and innovative offerings, find themselves at the forefront of a global food movement, leading to increased footfall and economic prosperity.

However, the embrace of globalization in street food comes with its set of challenges. Economic disparities can emerge as global influences may lead to increased costs of certain ingredients, impacting the profit margins of small-scale vendors. The pressure to align with international trends may pose challenges for traditional vendors who grapple with the need to innovate while preserving the authenticity that defines their culinary identity.

Moreover, the competitive landscape expands as globalization introduces a plethora of choices for consumers. Street food vendors must navigate this complexity by striking a balance between offering familiar local favorites and introducing innovative global creations. The challenge lies in managing this delicate equilibrium to remain economically viable while satisfying the evolving tastes of their customer base.

In the face of these challenges, street food entrepreneurs in India exhibit remarkable resilience, innovation, and adaptability. They leverage globalization not just as a challenge but as an opportunity for growth and expansion.

To navigate economic challenges, street food vendors often diversify their offerings. This might involve incorporating international flavors into their menus or introducing unique fusions that cater to a broad spectrum of tastes. This diversification not only attracts a wider customer base but also ensures adaptability in the face of changing culinary trends.

In the digital age, street food vendors are increasingly leveraging technology to reach a broader audience. Social media platforms serve as powerful marketing tools, allowing vendors to showcase their culinary creations to a global audience. Online delivery services enable customers to enjoy street food specialties from the comfort of their homes, further expanding the economic reach of small-scale entrepreneurs.

Recognizing the importance of community support, many street food vendors actively engage with local residents and businesses. Building a loyal customer base fosters economic sustainability and resilience against external economic shocks. Additionally, embracing sustainable practices, such as sourcing local ingredients and minimizing food waste, not only aligns with global trends but also enhances the economic viability of street food businesses.

In the concluding sections, we will delve deeper into specific case studies and success stories that highlight the economic dynamism of street food entrepreneurship in India. Through these narratives, we gain a nuanced understanding of how economic opportunities and challenges intertwine in the ever- evolving landscape of street food economics.

The future of street food in the era of globalization holds exciting prospects and innovative trends that are poised to shape the culinary landscape of India.

Embracing Plant-Based and Sustainable Options

As environmental consciousness grows globally, street food vendors in India are increasingly exploring plant-based and sustainable options. From vegan versions of traditional favorites to innovative plant-based street food creations, vendors are aligning their offerings with the rising demand for sustainable and ethical food choices. This shift not only addresses environmental concerns but also caters to the evolving preferences of health-conscious consumers.

Technology Integration for Accessibility

The integration of technology is set to play a pivotal role in the future of street food. Mobile apps and online platforms for ordering, delivery, and payment are becoming more prevalent, making street food more accessible to a wider audience. This trend not only caters to the convenience-seeking urban population but also opens up new avenues for street food vendors to expand their reach and thrive in the digital age.

Culinary Cross-Pollination and Global Fusion

The fusion of global and local flavors is expected to continue evolving, creating culinary hybrids that delight the senses. Street food vendors, inspired by diverse global cuisines, will likely continue to experiment with creative combinations, offering consumers a taste of the world on a single plate. This culinary cross-pollination not only enriches the street food experience but also contributes to the global dialogue of flavors.

As we conclude this exploration, the global street food landscape in India emerges as a cultural symphony—a vibrant interplay of flavors, stories, and economic dynamics. Street food, once a local affair, has transcended geographical boundaries, becoming a dynamic force that reflects the interconnectedness of cultures in the era of globalization.

In the bustling streets of India, where the sizzle of grills mingles with the chatter of vendors and customers, street food becomes a tangible expression of cultural exchange. It is a celebration of diversity, an economic driver for entrepreneurs, and a canvas for culinary creativity. Challenges notwithstanding, the future holds exciting prospects where sustainability, innovation, and a global culinary dialogue converge to shape the street food experience.

As we navigate the ever-evolving global street food tapestry, let us savor not only the flavors on our plates but also the stories, traditions, and entrepreneurial spirit that make street food an enduring and cherished aspect of our culinary heritage. The journey continues, and the streets beckon with the promise of new culinary adventures, reflecting the dynamic fusion of global influences and local traditions.

Section 10

POLICY AND REGULATION OF STREET FOOD

The genesis of street food is deeply intertwined with the fabric of human history and societal evolution. Originating as a response to urbanization, street food has evolved from a simple means of sustenance to a global culinary phenomenon. Its roots delve into the communal spirit of local markets, where vendors skillfully transform humble ingredients into savory treasures. Yet, as the popularity of street food has soared, so too has the need for regulatory frameworks that govern its practices.

Amidst the aromatic allure and bustling energy, the importance of evaluating policies for street food vendors cannot be overstated. Beyond mere gastronomic pleasure, street food is a socio-economic force, contributing to livelihoods, cultural heritage, and community identity. Recognizing this, the study places a spotlight on the pivotal role of policies in shaping the destiny of street food. It endeavors to shed light on how these regulations impact economic viability, cultural preservation, public health, and the entrepreneurial spirit within the industry.

As we embark on this flavorful journey through the regulatory landscape of street food, we delve into the intricacies, challenges, and triumphs that define this culinary realm. The following sections will dissect the historical evolution of street food policies, scrutinize the licensing systems, and narrate real-life stories that encapsulate the struggles and successes of street food vendors navigating the intricate maze of regulations. Through this exploration, we aim to contribute not only to the academic understanding of street food governance but also to the ongoing discourse surrounding the sustenance of this dynamic and cherished facet of urban life.

In the rich tapestry of Indian culinary traditions, street food stands as an indomitable pillar, intertwining flavors, aromas, and a vibrant street culture. The literature on the anthropology of street food in India delves into the socio-cultural dimensions that make street food an integral part of daily life. Studies highlight the ritualistic aspect of street food consumption, often rooted in community gatherings and celebrations. The bustling markets of Delhi, Mumbai's street corners, and the vibrant street food stalls in Kolkata collectively narrate a story of gastronomic diversity deeply embedded in the Indian way of life.

Scholarly perspectives explore how street food transcends nourishment to become a cultural artifact that binds communities. It is not merely about the culinary experience but also about the shared memories, rituals, and traditions associated with street food. The literature emphasizes the need for regulatory frameworks that appreciate and preserve this cultural significance while addressing contemporary challenges.

Within the Indian context, street food plays a pivotal role in community building, forging connections that extend beyond the culinary realm. Literature reveals that street food vendors are not just purveyors of snacks but often serve as community anchors. The informal relationships between vendors and customers create a sense of familiarity and belonging, transforming street corners into communal spaces.

The review of studies highlights the role of street food in building community identity. Street food becomes a shared narrative, reflecting the diverse cultural landscapes within India. Whether it's the chaat in Delhi, pav bhaji in Mumbai, or puchka in Kolkata, each street food item carries a cultural history that resonates with locals and visitors alike. The literature suggests that regulations need to consider and support these community-building aspects, ensuring that policies do not inadvertently disrupt the social fabric that street food weaves.

In the labyrinthine lanes of Old Delhi, where history whispers through centuries-old structures, the chaat vendors stand as modern-day storytellers. One such vendor, Rajesh, has been crafting delectable plates of spicy aloo chaat for over two decades. His cart, a colorful spectacle, is not just a culinary haven but a hub of community chatter.

As customers gather around Rajesh's cart, exchanging stories and laughter, the true essence of street food unfolds. The sizzle of potatoes in the pan harmonizes with the symphony of diverse languages, creating a microcosm of Delhi's cultural mosaic. Rajesh, with his deft hands and warm smile, is more than a vendor; he is a custodian of community memories.

However, regulatory challenges loom large. Rajesh, like many street food vendors in Old Delhi, navigates a maze of permits and inspections. The literature review contextualizes these challenges within the broader discussion on the need for regulatory frameworks that recognize and preserve the cultural and community dimensions of street food.

India's street food landscape, a dazzling array of flavors and traditions, is intertwined with a regulatory tapestry that mirrors the country's diverse cultural and economic fabric.

Mumbai's Dabbawalas: In Mumbai, the iconic dabbawalas exemplify a unique form of street food delivery. While not traditional vendors, their informal network operates without formal licensing. The city's regulatory stance recognizes their cultural significance, allowing them to thrive in the absence of conventional licensing.

Delhi's Chaat Wallahs: Delhi's vibrant street food scene, particularly the chaat wallahs in Old Delhi, navigates a more formalized regulatory framework. Licensing requirements exist, emphasizing food safety and hygiene. However, challenges persist, with vendors facing procedural complexities and occasional lapses in enforcement.

India's street food policies play a pivotal role in shaping the livelihoods of vendors across the country.

Urban Variances: Metropolitan areas like Mumbai and Delhi may showcase variations in regulatory enforcement. While Mumbai's informal networks coexist with limited interference, Delhi's more formalized system requires vendors to navigate regulatory hurdles.

Economic Implications: Licensing costs and procedural complexities impact the economic viability of vendors. In many cases, vendors, especially those in Delhi, face financial barriers, affecting their ability to comply with formal regulations.

Delhi's Licensing Framework: In Delhi, street food vendors are required to obtain licenses from municipal authorities. These licenses are intended to ensure adherence to hygiene standards and public health regulations. However, the process is often criticized for its complexity, leading to challenges in obtaining and renewing licenses.

Mumbai's Informal Networks: Mumbai's dabbawalas operate in a less formalized environment. While not subjected to traditional licensing requirements, they face a different set of challenges, including the need for coordination and adherence to informal norms to maintain their credibility.

Understanding the nuances of India's street food regulatory landscape is essential for addressing the unique challenges faced by vendors and fostering an environment that supports both cultural richness and economic sustainability. The subsequent sections will delve deeper into the on-the-ground realities faced by street food vendors in Indian cities, unraveling the stories of triumphs and struggles that define their journey within the regulatory framework.

Let's look at Maria's story. Maria, a determined street food vendor in the heart of Mumbai, embarked on her journey selling street tacos, weaving her way through the intricate regulatory landscape of the city.

In a vibrant corner of South Mumbai, Maria set up her humble taco stand, infusing the air with the aroma of spices and sizzling meats. The allure of her street tacos soon gained popularity among locals and tourists alike, becoming a staple for those seeking an authentic taste of Mumbai's street food.

Maria, however, faced the challenges of navigating Mumbai's formalized licensing system. Obtaining the necessary permits required a dance through bureaucratic hoops, testing her resilience. The costs associated with licensing posed financial hurdles, but Maria's determination propelled her forward.

Despite the regulatory hurdles, Maria's commitment to quality and adherence to hygiene standards not only ensured the longevity of her business but also garnered trust among her customers. Her story is one of triumph over adversity, showcasing how resilience, coupled with an understanding of regulatory necessities, can lead to a thriving street food venture.

Now let's look at one more story of a boy named Ahmed.

Ahmed, an ambitious vendor in the bustling streets of Mumbai, faced the labyrinth of regulatory complexities in his quest to bring his culinary delights to the masses.

Hailing from Cairo, Ahmed brought with him the flavors of Egyptian street food to the diverse culinary landscape of Mumbai. His falafel wraps and koshari quickly gained popularity, attracting a loyal customer base.

However, Ahmed found himself entangled in the complexities of Mumbai's licensing system. The formalized approach, while aiming to uphold hygiene standards, presented procedural challenges. Ahmed struggled to navigate the bureaucracy, encountering delays and uncertainties in obtaining the required permits.

The regulatory hurdles took a toll on Ahmed's business. Delays in approvals affected his ability to operate consistently, impacting both his revenue and customer base. Ahmed's story illuminates how regulatory mazes, if not streamlined, can hinder the growth of promising ventures and stifle culinary diversity.

These real-life stories within the Indian street food context echo the broader narrative of triumphs and struggles within the regulatory landscape. The experiences of Maria and Ahmed offer insights into the impact of regulations on vendor livelihoods, the complexities of compliance, and the dynamics of informal ventures. As we delve deeper into the shadows and highlights of street food entrepreneurship, the subsequent sections will explore the broader implications of these stories for the Indian regulatory framework and the vibrant street food culture it seeks to govern.

Economic Resilience of Street Food: Street food, as a micro- entrepreneurial endeavor, is a robust generator of employment. Maria's success in Mumbai exemplifies how overcoming regulatory challenges can lead to sustained employment opportunities. The economic ripple effect extends to suppliers, delivery personnel, and various support services, fostering a network of employment within the street food ecosystem.

Ahmed's Struggles in Mumbai: Ahmed's challenges highlight the vulnerability of employment generation within the street food sector when faced with regulatory hurdles. Delays in licensing approvals can disrupt business operations, affecting not only the vendor but also the individuals employed in the supply chain. The economic impact is felt not just by the vendor but also by those dependent on the street food ecosystem for their livelihoods.

Economic policies related to street food regulation must strike a delicate balance. While ensuring hygiene standards and public health, policymakers need to consider the economic implications for vendors. Exploring avenues for reducing financial barriers, streamlining licensing procedures, and offering financial support can contribute to a more economically inclusive street food sector.

Policies should aim not only to regulate but also to facilitate inclusive economic growth. This involves recognizing the economic resilience of street food and creating frameworks that nurture entrepreneurship. Initiatives such as microfinance support, training programs, and simplified licensing procedures can enhance economic opportunities for street food vendors.

Street food is not just about the flavors on the plate; it is a living testament to cultural heritage and diversity. The assessment of how regulations impact the cultural preservation of street food explores the delicate balance between standardization and the authenticity of culinary traditions.

Cultural policies within the street food sector should be adaptive, recognizing the diverse culinary traditions embedded in the fabric of Indian society. Regulatory frameworks need to accommodate this diversity, allowing for regional variations and the evolution of culinary practices while ensuring basic standards of safety and hygiene.

In crafting cultural preservation policies, involving communities and vendors in the decision-making process is crucial. Recognizing the role of street food vendors as custodians of cultural heritage can lead to more inclusive and culturally sensitive regulatory approaches.

The economic viability of vendors, employment generation, and the preservation of cultural diversity are interwoven elements that demand a nuanced and adaptive regulatory framework. As we unravel the impact of regulations on the vibrant street food culture of India, the subsequent sections will delve into the community and social aspects, exploring how regulations shape the relationships and dynamics within street food spaces.

The government plays a pivotal role in shaping the regulatory landscape for street food vendors. Exploring the perspectives of government officials responsible for street food regulation offers valuable insights into the considerations, challenges, and aspirations that guide policymaking in this domain.

Engaging in interviews with key government officials, such as municipal authorities and health inspectors, provides a deeper understanding of their perspectives on street food regulation.

Views on Current Policies: Government officials acknowledge the importance of street food regulations in ensuring public health and safety. Formalized licensing systems in major cities like Delhi and Mumbai are viewed as necessary for maintaining hygiene standards. Officials express satisfaction with the existing frameworks that aim to strike a balance between formality and cultural diversity.

Challenges in Implementation: Government officials, however, highlight challenges in the effective implementation of regulations. Enforcement disparities, procedural complexities, and resource constraints contribute to gaps in ensuring consistent compliance. Recognizing these challenges, officials express a commitment to addressing them for a more robust regulatory environment.

One of the key challenges faced by street food vendors revolves around the complexity and time-consuming nature of licensing procedures. Streamlining these processes is essential for fostering a more inclusive and efficient regulatory environment.

Implementing user-friendly, online platforms for license applications and renewals can significantly reduce the bureaucratic burden on vendors. Digitalization ensures transparency and expedites the entire licensing process. Reevaluate and simplify the documentation required for licensing. Clear guidelines and checklists can aid vendors in preparing the necessary paperwork, reducing confusion and potential delays.

Implementing a comprehensive set of reforms encompassing streamlined licensing processes, community engagement, and support mechanisms can nurture a sustainable street food ecosystem. These recommendations aim to balance regulatory objectives with the economic, cultural, and social dynamics inherent in the vibrant world of Indian street food. As we conclude this exploration, the subsequent sections will recapitulate key findings and emphasize the collective responsibility of stakeholders in shaping the future of street food regulation.

The integration of technology stands as a powerful catalyst for revolutionizing regulatory processes for street food vendors. Embracing digital solutions has the potential to streamline operations, enhance transparency, and promote regulatory compliance.

Implementing centralized online platforms for license applications and renewals can significantly reduce administrative burdens for vendors. Such platforms provide a convenient and transparent avenue for vendors to engage with regulatory processes, reducing paperwork and processing times.

Incorporate digital inspection systems that leverage mobile applications. Health inspectors equipped with digital tools can conduct real-time inspections, ensuring immediate feedback and facilitating more efficient monitoring of compliance.

In conclusion, the exploration of street food regulation, sustainability, and future trends underscores the need for a balanced and adaptive approach. As India's street food landscape continues to evolve, the collective responsibility of government bodies, vendors, communities, and technology becomes paramount in shaping a resilient and vibrant street food ecosystem.

Balanced regulations are essential for harmonizing economic growth, cultural preservation, and public health objectives. The recommendations put forth, including streamlined licensing, community engagement, and support mechanisms, form a holistic framework for achieving this balance.

As the street food landscape evolves, the need for continued research and policy advocacy becomes apparent. Ongoing efforts should focus on understanding emerging trends, evaluating the impact of implemented reforms, and advocating for policies that foster sustainability and inclusivity.

The journey toward a thriving street food ecosystem is dynamic and multifaceted. By embracing innovation, collaboration, and a commitment to balance, stakeholders can collectively contribute to the resilience and sustainability of India's rich street food culture.

TOP 10 STREET FOOD LOCATIONS OF INDIA

Volcano Pani Puri Of Surat

Location: Aayush Panipuri Center, Opp. Jayesh Medical Store, Udhna 3 Rasta, Udhna Udhyog Nagar, Udhna, Surat, Gujarat

Nestled in the bustling streets of Surat, 'Aayush Panipuri Center' has emerged as a culinary phenomenon, captivating millions of internet users across India. The stall's claim to fame is the innovative "Volcano Pani Puri," a sensory delight that goes beyond the traditional charm of street food. The eruption of tangy tamarind water, spicy chutneys, and aromatic spices within delicate puris has turned this unassuming stall into a national sensation. As social media buzzes with videos showcasing the meticulous craft behind each miniature volcano, Aayush Panipuri Center has become a pilgrimage for food enthusiasts eager to experience the explosive joy of this unique creation. In the ever-evolving landscape of Indian street food, Aayush Panipuri Center stands as a testament to the transformative power of innovation and the enduring allure of a culinary spectacle that transcends local boundaries.

Rajma Chawal of Jammu

Location: Khajuria's Food Mall, Miran Sahib, near Bhagat Singh Park, Jammu, Jammu and Kashmir

In the heart of Jammu, 'Khajuria Dharna' stands as a culinary haven, celebrated for its soul-satisfying Rajma Chawal. This unassuming eatery has become synonymous with the rich and flavorful indulgence of this quintessential North Indian dish. Locals and visitors alike flock to Khajuria Dharna to savor the aromatic blend of kidney beans in a savory gravy, served alongside perfectly cooked rice. The establishment has earned its fame not through extravagant decor but through the time- honored tradition of crafting a bowl of comfort that resonates with the essence of home-cooked meals. A pilgrimage site for Rajma Chawal enthusiasts, Khajuria Dharna invites all to partake in the simple joy of a hearty meal that encapsulates the warmth and hospitality of Jammu's culinary heritage.

Vada Pav of Mumbai

Location: Ashok Vada Pav Off Cadel Road, Kirti College Lane, Prabhadevi, Mumbai

Nestled in the bustling streets of Dadar, Mumbai, Ashok Vada Pav has earned its stripes as a culinary icon, celebrated for its delectable Vada Pav. This humble eatery has become a go-to spot for locals and visitors seeking the quintessential Mumbai street food experience. Ashok Vada Pav's fame lies in its simplicity and consistency, serving crispy, flavorful potato fritters sandwiched between soft pav bread, garnished with chutneys and spices. The iconic red and white board bearing the stall's name is a beacon for Vada Pav enthusiasts, inviting them to indulge in this savory delight that encapsulates the spirit of Mumbai's vibrant street food culture.

Dabeli of Ahmedabad

Location: Ujala Circle, makarba, Ahmedabad - 380051 (Near Bus Stop)

In the heart of culinary delights in Gujarat, Karnavati Vada Pav has emerged as the go-to destination for a savory experience, particularly renowned for its flavorful Dabeli. This humble eatery, celebrated for its authenticity and taste, has become a favorite among locals and visitors alike. The star of the show is the Dabeli – a spiced potato mixture encased in a pav, garnished with a melange of chutneys, sev, and pomegranate seeds. Karnavati Vada Pav's legacy is not just in crafting a delicious snack but in providing a sensory journey that captures the essence of Gujarat's rich street food heritage. With every bite, patrons indulge in the perfect harmony of spices, textures, and flavors, making Karnavati Vada Pav a true ambassador of Dabeli delights.

Basket Aloo tikki of Lucknow

Location: 51, Mahatma Gandhi Marg, Sushanpura, Hazratganj, Lucknow, Uttar Pradesh 226001

In the heart of Lucknow's culinary landscape, Royal Cafe stands tall as a gastronomic haven, with its Basket Aloo Chaat emerging as a crowned jewel. This famed eatery has mastered the art of creating an exquisite blend of flavors and textures in a simple yet captivating street food delight. The Basket Aloo Chaat, served in a crispy edible basket, features perfectly spiced and roasted potatoes, adorned with a symphony of chutneys, yogurt, and spices. Royal Cafe's culinary prowess lies not only in crafting a visually appealing dish but also in delivering a burst of authentic Lucknowi flavors that dance on the taste buds. As a beloved symbol of the city's rich street food heritage, Royal Cafe's Basket Aloo Chaat beckons both locals and tourists to savor the royal experience in every delightful bite.

Chole Bhature of Delhi

Location: Sita Ram Diwan Chand,2246, Near Imperial Cinema,
Paharganj, New Delhi.

Located in the lively streets of Delhi, Sita Ram Diwan Chand has earned its reputation as a culinary gem, celebrated for its delectable Chole Bhature. This iconic establishment has become a go-to spot, attracting food enthusiasts from all walks of life. The spotlight shines on their Chole Bhature – a delightful combination of airy, deep-fried bread paired with a flavorful and spicy chickpea curry. Sita Ram Diwan Chand's legacy extends beyond the mastery of its recipe; it encapsulates the essence of a classic Delhi street food experience, invoking a sense of nostalgia. Each crispy bite and every spoonful of their flavorful curry transports patrons on a culinary journey through the rich flavors of North India. Sita Ram Diwan Chand remains a beloved destination, cherished by both locals and visitors, embodying the timeless allure of Delhi's culinary treasures.

Misal Pav of Pune

Location: Malhar misal, Aundh - Ravet BRTS Road Near Kokane Market Jagtap Dairy Chowk, Rahatani, Pimpri-Chinchwad, Maharashtra 411017

In the bustling streets of Pune, Malhar Misal Pav stands as a spice haven, celebrated for its signature Misal Pav. This local gem has become synonymous with fiery flavors and authentic Maharashtrian taste. The Misal, a spicy sprout curry, is served with soft pav bread and garnished with an array of crunchy namkeen, farsan, and coriander. Malhar's Misal Pav is not just a dish; it's a sensory adventure that captures the essence of Pune's vibrant street food culture. With its aromatic spices and bold taste, Malhar Misal Pav has secured its place as a beloved destination, drawing both locals and visitors to savor the bold flavors of Maharashtra in every spicy bite

Samosa of Kanpur

Location: 'Munna Samosa', 109, 80-A, Near Balaji Mandir,
Sisamau Bazar, Nehru Nagar, Ram Bagh, Kanpur, Uttar
Pradesh 208012

In Kanpur's culinary landscape, 'Munna Samosa' proudly stands as a symbol of the city's gastronomic excellence. Renowned as "Kanpur Ki Shaan" or the pride of Kanpur, this esteemed eatery has become synonymous with its irresistible samosas. Munna Samosa distinguishes itself not only through the impeccable crispiness of its samosas but also by offering a diverse range of fillings, including spicy potatoes, savory peas, and lentils. Locals and visitors alike flock to Munna Samosa, seeking an authentic taste of Kanpur's street food culture. With each savory bite, Munna Samosa narrates the story of Kanpur's culinary legacy, solidifying its status as a beloved destination for those in search of the city's pride and gastronomic distinction.

Pyaaz Kachori of Jodhpur

Location: Rajasthan Sweets & Restaurant, 93M8+2M3, Daijar, Mandore, Jodhpur, Restaurant

In the enchanting city of Jodhpur, 'Rajasthan Namkeen Bhandara' reigns supreme as the go-to destination for the iconic Pyaaz Kachori. This beloved eatery has become synonymous with the rich flavors and culinary heritage of Rajasthan. The Pyaaz Kachori, a delightful fried pastry filled with spiced onion stuffing, is a testament to the traditional Rajasthani taste that captivates locals and visitors alike. Rajasthan Namkeen Bhandara is not just a place to savor a snack; it's a cultural journey through the streets of Jodhpur encapsulated in every crunchy and savory bite. With its aromatic spices and perfected recipes, this establishment has rightfully earned its fame, making it a cherished spot for those seeking the essence of Rajasthan's delectable street food offerings.

Dosa of Bengaluru

*Location: Central Tiffin Room, 7th Cross, Margosa Road,
Malleshwaram, Bangalore*

Situated amidst the vibrant streets of Bengaluru, the
'Central Tiffin Room' (CTR) is a renowned establishment,
celebrated for its exquisite dosas. This iconic eatery
is synonymous with South Indian culinary mastery,
particularly for its delectable dosa creations. CTR's
signature benne (butter) dosa is a crispy delight generously
adorned with butter and filled with a flavorful potato
mixture. Locals and visitors alike flock to CTR, drawn by
the authentic taste of Bengaluru's cherished dosa tradition.
Seamlessly blending tradition with taste, CTR has solidified
its status as a revered institution, beckoning patrons to
relish the essence of Bengaluru's rich gastronomic heritage
in each delightful bite.

ABOUT FOODITY

Meet the culinary visionaries behind the tantalizing exploration of India's street food scene in "Beyond Brick and Mortar." The creative force driving this gastronomic odyssey is the dynamic team Foodity—India's foremost top-1% street food venture. Headed by serial entrepreneur Aditya S Kapur, renowned for pioneering solution-led businesses, the team is completed by the seasoned designer Vrinda Arora and the creative researcher Samya Modi.

Aditya S Kapur, a maverick in the entrepreneurial realm, has carved a niche for himself with a knack for transforming ideas into successful ventures. His commitment to solution-oriented business approaches is evident in the groundbreaking initiatives he has championed.

Vrinda Arora, the design virtuoso, adds a visually enchanting layer to "Beyond Brick and Mortar." With a wealth of experience in design, Vrinda brings a keen eye for aesthetics, ensuring that the book not only captivates through its narrative but also through its visual journey.

Samya Modi, the creative researcher, is the driving force behind the book's immersive storytelling. With a passion for unearthing untold stories, Samya's meticulous research and creative flair bring the vibrant narratives of street vendors to life, making "Beyond Brick and Mortar" a compelling and authentic exploration of India's street food culture.

Together, the Foodity team blends business acumen, design expertise, and creative research to deliver a culinary masterpiece that goes beyond the plate, offering readers an insightful and immersive experience into the rich tapestry of India's street food market.